BENTLEY
FOUR-CYLINDER MODELS
In Detail

BENTLEY
FOUR-CYLINDER MODELS
In Detail

BY JAMES TAYLOR

Herridge & Sons

Acknowledgments

The author and the publisher are grateful to the Bentley Drivers' Club and their archivist Alan Bodfish for access to the club's archive, which provided many of the photographs reproduced in this book. Other photographs were kindly loaned by Tim Houlding, Bryan Goodman, the David Hodges collection, the author, Gregor Fisken and Bentley Motors. The specially commissioned colour photographs are by Simon Clay and Tom Wood, and thanks are due to the following for making their cars available for photography: Bentley Motors (EXP 2, 4½-litre supercharged 1930 Le Mans car), Andy Hall (3-litre Connaught tourer), Tim Houlding (3-litre Speed Model chassis), Tom Pasmore (3-litre HJ Mulliner saloon), Jens Pilo (3-litre Vanden Plas tourer), David Lawson (4½-litre Vanden Plas tourer), and James Medcalf (3-litre Speed Model Vanden Plas tourer, 3-litre 1926 Le Mans car, 4½-litre Tickford folding-head saloon).

Published in 2012 by
Herridge & Sons Ltd
Lower Forda, Shebbear,
Beaworthy, Devon EX21 5SY

© Copyright James Taylor 2012
Designed by Ray Leaning, MUSE Fine Art & Design

Special photography by Simon Clay and Tom
Wood

ISBN 978-1-906133-30-6
Printed in Singapore

Contents

Introduction

Vanden Plas certainly did body a large number of 3-litres as Sports four-seaters, but fortunately not all were green. The Vanden Plas records in fact show that this one, on Speed chassis TN 1563, originally had cream and red paint to go with its red fabric panels. Note the single door on the nearside: front seat passengers had to climb in over the body sides. The car is owned by Jens Pilo.

Whan my publisher Charles Herridge and I looked into the scope for books about vintage Bentleys, we both came to the same conclusion. The subject had been covered exhaustively over the years, and from several different angles – but there was nothing on the market which presented the subject in accessible form for the average motoring enthusiast. Many of the good books were sadly out of print (though available for very high prices on the second-hand market), and there were many others of a highly detailed nature which appealed only to the hard-core enthusiast.

Not surprisingly, then, I began my work on this book by devouring as much of the existing material as I could. In that, I was considerably helped by the library of the WO Bentley Foundation. Key among the books I found valuable in providing information were Bruce H Brown's

fascinating examination of *WO Bentley and the DFP*, Michael Frostick's *Bentley, Cricklewood to Crewe*, Nick Walker's *Coachwork on Vintage Bentleys*, and WO Bentley's own books, *WO, The autobiography of WO Bentley*, and *An Illustrated History of the Bentley Car*. Nobody writes about vintage Bentleys without first reading Michael Hay's *Bentley: The Vintage Years 1919-1931* and *Bentley Factory Cars, 1919-1931*, and I found them indispensable for their detailed research. Most interesting because of their wealth of illustrations were Johnnie Green's *Bentley, 50 Years of the Marque* and Brian Smith's *Vanden Plas*. Nicholas Foulkes's *The Bentley Era* turned out to be an enjoyable look at a different aspect of the marque. I was lucky enough to find a copy of *The Technical Facts of the Vintage Bentley*, published by the Bentley Driver's Club, at an autojumble and made good use of its technical detail. Finally, I found completely invaluable the immediate access to information on Robert McLellan's website, www.vintagebentleys.org.

You may well wonder why this book is devoted only to the four-cylinder cars and not to the complete range of Bentleys built between 1919 and 1931. The answer is quite simple: to put everything between the same pair of covers would have made the book impossibly expensive. My publisher and I agreed that the most sensible split of the material was between four-cylinder and six-cylinder cars, not least because the six-cylinders (6½-litre, Speed Six, 8-litre and 4-litre) are different from the four-cylinders in more ways than just the cylinder count. So the second part of this story appears in a companion volume entitled *Bentley Six-Cylinder Models in Detail*. This book has been made immeasurably more attractive and informative by the splendid colour photographs that Simon Clay has taken, and I am sure all its readers will join me in thanking him for illustrating my words so ably.

James Taylor
Oxfordshire, November 2011

Now preserved by Bentley Motors, UU 5872 is one of the supercharged Birkin team cars, built on chassis number HB 3403.

Chapter One

Formative Years

The years immediately after the end of the Great War in 1918 were a fascinating period for the British motor industry. They were times of great optimism, when a number of men who had encountered automotive engineering during their war service decided to try their hand at building cars. Few were successful in the longer term, although the atmosphere of the times favoured their efforts as the British people looked to a future without the hardships of the war years. Just around the corner were the Roaring Twenties, a riot of optimism and new ideas and – sadly – just beyond them were the Wall Street Crash and the attendant Depression.

It was into this period that the Bentley motor car was introduced. It rode on the optimism of the times, perhaps picking up on a post-war patriotism which was fuelled by Britain's emergence from the war on the winning side. In the motor car industry, America might still hold the lead but Britain was determined to topple the French from second place. Right seemed to be on the British side, and WO Bentley was one of those who believed it was.

Walter Owen Bentley was born on 16 September 1888 as the youngest of nine children, to a wealthy middle-class family living in London. Like most of his siblings, he was usually known by his initials rather than by his full name and, as he appears not to have liked the name Walter, that suited him well. Like so many children of his background at that time,

WO was sent at the age of 13 to boarding school, and between 1902 and 1905 he attended Clifton College in Bristol, a leading public school known for its progressive approach to science subjects. Here, his parents no doubt expected him to learn the attitudes and some of the skills that would enable him to become a leader among his fellow men.

Many people in WO's position settled for the traditional options of the civil service, the military, or the professions, but this was a time when engineering offered some exciting challenges, and when WO left Clifton in July 1905, he went to study engineering theory at King's College in London. Disappointed by the absence of any practical element in the course, he decided to leave and get the experience he wanted with the Great Northern Railway at Doncaster.

Trains and taxi-cabs

WO joined the GNR as a premium apprentice, which meant his family had paid for the training and that he immediately enjoyed certain privileges among his fellow apprentices. Railway engineering famously encouraged a mind-set in which items were manufactured to be strong and to last, and it is hard not to imagine that much of this attitude rubbed off on the young man during the six years of his work with the company.

Initially, WO used a bicycle in Doncaster, but he soon showed an interest in the motorcycles that some of his fellow apprentices owned and decided he had to have one. That first motor-cycle was a Quadrant, and he gradually moved on to better and more powerful machines. He entered racing and touring events, too, and before long his older brothers HM (Horace) and AW (Arthur) were touring with him. The Bentley brothers joined various motorcycling clubs, and in 1907 AW persuaded WO to join him for the Motor Cycling Club's notoriously difficult London-Edinburgh reliability trial. Despite mechanical difficulties during the event, WO managed to reach the finish on time and won himself a gold medal. Two years later, he entered his Speed King motorcycle in the Tourist Trophy race on the Isle of Man but crashed and, unable to repair his mount, was obliged to retire.

These activities were again important in influencing the later course of WO's life. They revealed and nurtured a love of competitive motorsport which would remain with him and would influence the destiny of the Bentley motor car company. At the same time, this period saw him become gradually disillusioned with his prospects in the railway industry, while the possibility of working within the motor industry began to seem both more attractive and more exciting. So, through a contact at *The Autocar*, he secured an interview with the National Motor Cab Company in Hammersmith, London, and was given a job overseeing the everyday operation and maintenance of the cabs, which were mostly of Unic manufacture. This gave him a valuable insight into everyday reliability problems, and no doubt contributed to his concern with that aspect of motor car engineering in later years. Around 1910, he bought his first car, a 9hp Riley dating from 1906-1907; a year later, he moved on to a French-built Sizaire-Naudin.

The DFP period

The year 1912 turned out to be a turning-point. Another of the Bentley brothers, Leonard (LH), was looking for somewhere to invest money after selling off his unprofitable farming business towards the end of 1911, and HM spotted a classified advertisement in *The Times* which seemed to fit the bill. A London company called Lecoq & Fernie was looking for an investor to take a major share in its business of importing the French DFP, Buchet and La Licorne cars.

After a family discussion, it was WO rather than LH Bentley who joined them, paying £2000 and becoming a director in January 1912. Just a month later, HM Bentley invested another £2000 to buy the remaining shares in the company, and the original owners stepped down. By June 1912, the business had been renamed Bentley & Bentley. It took over the DFP showrooms in Hanover Street, near Oxford Street in London's West End; HM Bentley took over the sales side of the business and established his office here.

Of the three French marques, the DFP showed the most promise, and Bentley & Bentley quickly dropped the other two. They imported the cars from France in chassis form, and arranged for their bodies to be constructed by Harrison's, of Stanhope Street in London's Camden Town area. The bodies were trimmed by another company, JH Easter of New Street Mews (since re-named Chagford Street) near the top end of Baker Street in Marylebone, and Bentley & Bentley rented from Easter's a coach-house further down the mews. They turned this into the DFP service station and workshops, and it was here that WO was based.

The Bentley brothers had no intention of allowing the business to stagnate, as the previous proprietors had done. At an early stage they arranged for a DFP mechanic called Leroux to be sent from France and attached to their London workshops so that they could develop the car. Of the three DFP models they imported – the 10/12hp, 12/15hp, and 16/22hp – WO believed that the 2-litre 12/15 offered the most

Bentley & Bentley imported the French DFP in the years immediately before the Great War, and recognised the beneficial value of racing success on sales. This is WO himself at the start of the 1914 Tourist Trophy race, in which his sixth placing did DFP sales a power of good. (BDC)

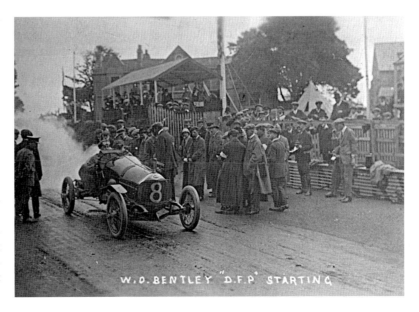

W.O. BENTLEY "D.F.P" STARTING

opportunity for tuning, and in May 1912 he and Leroux set about improving its performance. First, they raised its compression ratio, and by June they were getting 70mph out of what had been a 55mph motor car.

This was no small achievement, but it was of little value unless the buying public knew about it. WO and his brother recognised that the most effective way of attracting the publicity that generated sales was to enter a car in competition – and to be successful with it. Their first competition success with the DFP, with WO at the wheel, was at the Aston Rowant hillclimb in Oxfordshire on 12 May.

Just over a year later, there occurred an event which, in retrospect, turned out to be one of the most important in WO's life. In late July 1913, he visited the DFP factory at Courbevoie, just north-west of Paris, with the intention of persuading the company to raise the compression ratio and modify the carburettor and induction system on 12/15 models for the British market. On the desk of Auguste Doriot, the D of DFP, he spotted an ornamental paperweight – a miniature piston cast in aluminium. This set him thinking, and before long he persuaded Doriot to have a set of full-size aluminium pistons cast in France to suit the 12/15's engine.

The results when these were fitted were astonishing. The lightweight pistons allowed the engine to rev more freely and to develop even more power, and by autumn 1913 WO was confident that he could gain the sort of publicity that Bentley & Bentley wanted if he aimed to take some class records at the Brooklands race

track. He had a 12/15 chassis fitted with a special streamlined single-seat racing body by Harrison's, and during September he took every single Class B record at the track. In November 1913, he broke all those records again with the car, and then in February 1914 he set new records for the third time.

This caused quite a stir, and the DFP quickly became highly regarded in sporting circles. DFP owners soon came to include Woolf Barnato, Sir Henry (Tim) Birkin, Frank Clement, Sammy Davis and John Duff, all of whom would later have important roles to play in the story of the Bentley motor car. As for WO, he now entered an example in the Isle of Man Tourist Trophy race in June 1914 and gained a lot more valuable press coverage when he brought the car home in sixth place. True, there were only six finishers, but many of the original starters had been forced to retire. The DFP had also been by far the smallest-engined car in the event and had put in a remarkably trouble-free run over the 600 miles and two days of the event.

Convinced of the merits of his redeveloped engine, WO proposed a new model which DFP duly put into production. With aluminium pistons and dual-plug ignition for reliability, the new 12/15 Speed Model (often wrongly called a 12/40, a name that was not in use before 1920) became available in 1914. It was Bentley & Bentley's great misfortune that the outbreak of war in France that autumn put a temporary end to their business of importing French cars.

Aero engines and tanks

WO joined up for the duration, volunteering for the Royal Naval Volunteer Reserve. However, he soon found himself seconded to the Technical Department of the new Royal Naval Air Service, where his knowledge of engines was clearly expected to prove useful. Among his earliest jobs were attachments to Rolls-Royce and Sunbeam, where he convinced senior management of the benefits of aluminium pistons. He was then sent to a company called Gwynne's of Chiswick, just west of London, to sort out problems with the French-designed Clerget 9B rotary aero engines which they were then building under licence.

Both the RNAS and the Royal Flying Corps were at this stage relying on these engines in their Sopwith Camels, but the Clerget engines had a severely limited life. The biggest problem

WO probably cringed at having his full name engraved on the reverse of his 1914 Tourist Trophy medal, but he could hardly have complained. The original medal still exists, in the hands of the Bentley Drivers' Club. (BDC)

(as with all rotary engines) was an uneven rate of cylinder expansion: the front of each cylinder was kept cool by the airstream, but the rear of the cylinder was not and therefore expanded more quickly. A small gasket-like component called an obturator ring was supposed to take care of sealing problems which these different rates of expansion caused, but was failing to do so. When it failed, the engine seized and the plane went down with its unlucky pilot.

WO made a number of attempts to improve the obturator ring, but encountered difficulties at Gwynne's, who did not welcome the disruption that these modifications caused to their production of the Clerget engine. So in March 1916, WO seems to have made clear to Commander Wilfred Briggs, his superior at the RNAS Technical Board, that a complete redesign of the engine was needed. He was initially given permission to make a single cylinder in aluminium with a cast-iron liner shrunk-fitted into it and to try this out on a Clerget engine whose other eight cylinders were to standard production specification.

The results convinced Briggs that WO had the ability to design his own aero engine. Briggs also knew that the Humber works in Coventry was being under-utilised as far as the war effort was concerned. He arranged for WO to be sent there and for the Humber people to give him the assistance he needed to get his ideas for a new engine into production. An interesting aside from this period is that WO could clearly see (or was persuaded to see) the potential commercial benefit of his ideas about aluminium pistons. In June 1916, the Aerolite Pistons Company was incorporated to take over the Bentley & Bentley piston interests. Its sole director in the beginning was AHMJ Ward, a third director of Bentley & Bentley who was married to Edith, sister of WO and HM. The Bentley brothers presumably kept their distance because both were serving in the armed forces at the time, but both added their names as directors in April 1919 after the war was over.

At Humber, WO initially designed a larger and more powerful engine than the Clerget, but Briggs encouraged him to focus on an engine that could act as a direct replacement for it. The result was the AR1 engine, its initials standing for Admiralty Rotary; after relatively few had been built, the name was changed to BR1, those initials standing for Bentley Rotary. The engine

From June 1915, WO enlisted for the duration in the Royal Naval Volunteer Reserve. The opportunities that the war afforded him to exploit his engineering talent underpinned his later success with Bentley cars. This photograph, showing him in Naval uniform, dates from the time of his war service.

(BDC)

was very much a development of the Clerget, featuring aluminium pistons running in aluminium cylinder barrels with cast-iron liners; with a longer stroke, it put out 150hp as against the Clerget's 130hp. It was also reliable and considerably cheaper to build. However, production at the Humber factory was never enough to meet the demand. As a result, although the BR1 was standardised for Camels delivered to the RNAS, the Clerget engine remained in production to meet the needs of the Royal Flying Corps. In the meantime it had been modified along the lines that WO had suggested; these later engines were known as the LS (Long Stroke) types and were rated at 140bhp.

The success of the BR1 earned WO a considerable reputation, and towards the end of 1916 he was asked to take a look at the engine of the then-new tank, a project with which the RNAS at this stage had an involvement. WO dutifully modified a British-built Daimler tank engine; tank historian David Fletcher explains that he raised the compression ratio and fitted aluminium pistons, twin Zenith carburettors and a lighter flywheel. The result was 125bhp at 1400rpm instead of 105bhp.

In this case, however, WO's efforts were less successful – though through no fault of his own. The Bentley-modified engine delivered more power than the rest of the tank's drivetrain could handle, and its association with a doomed petrol-electric transmission did its reputation no

bility. In *An Illustrated History of the Bentley Car*, he wrote of his sense of responsibility to the Naval pilots: "I was therefore three times as thorough as I might otherwise have been: I felt that the ghosts of men I had known who had been killed in combat or by accident through the unreliability of their machines were standing above me."

New ideas

Back in London at the war's end, the 30-year-old Captain Bentley (his rank had presumably changed when the RNAS was absorbed into the RAF in April 1918) and his older brother HM (now a Colonel after his war service) resumed their agency work with DFP cars, but WO already knew what he wanted to do next. Developing existing designs was all very well, and he had done that successfully with both the DFP car and the Clerget aero engine, but as a creative engineer he wanted to develop his own designs. He wanted to develop his own car.

So he made use of some of the friendships he had made during the war years, and persuaded two engineers he respected to join him in his new venture. The two were FT Burgess from Humber and HF (Harry) Varley, who had been an engine designer with Vauxhall. On Saturday, 18 January 1919, a bare two months after the Armistice had brought an end to the Great War on 11 November 1918, Bentley Motors Ltd was established as a company (it would be wound up and re-established in July for reasons which are still far from transparent). The three men began drawing up plans for the new Bentley car two days later on the Monday morning, working out of the Bentley & Bentley office at 16 Conduit Street in the fashionable Mayfair district of London.

They seem to have had a trusting, almost naïve belief that financial backers for their new venture would be found somewhere. In the meantime, HM Bentley did his best to drum up money for the new company by continuing to sell DFP cars from the Bentley & Bentley premises in Hanover Street nearby. At this stage the lack of proper finance was not a deterrent, and WO probably had at the back of his mind the notion that he would in due course be granted some cash for his aero engine work by the Commission for Awards to Inventors. (When it came, it was for £8000.) Besides, they had more interesting things to do than to worry about money.

favours. However, some of the Bentley-modified engines did see use in Supply tanks, where the transmission was not subjected to the same stresses as that of tanks used in battle.

His next task was to prepare a second and larger rotary engine for production. Based on the same principles as the BR1, this was the engine he had drawn up first and was known as the BR2. However, it did not enter production until spring 1918, just a few months before the war came to an end. Although this 230hp engine (later uprated to 245hp) was no less impressive than the BR1, it saw service mainly in the early 1920s at a time when Britain was no longer at war. Humber were unable to handle BR2 production alongside that of the BR1, and so although they contributed some common components to its manufacture, BR2 manufacture was co-ordinated by the Daimler factory in Coventry. However, it was at Humber that WO had made a number of valuable contacts. Notable among them was the company's chief designer, FT (Fred) Burgess, who shared WO's enthusiasm for motor racing and had designed the 1914 Humber TT cars as well as driven one of them in that race.

WO's wartime work with aero engines had been vitally important to the nation as well as to his own development as an engineer. For the former, he was rewarded with an MBE, which he received in January 1919. For the latter, it is clear that the most important lesson he learned and carried forward was the importance of relia-

Designing and building a brand-new car from scratch was an enormous undertaking, even in 1919 when designs were so much simpler than they are today. Almost nothing was available off the shelf, apart from such items as carburettors, lighting, wire wheels and magnetos, and so, after the design had been turned into blueprints, the manufacture of components had to be arranged with a variety of specialist suppliers. It would be the same almost to the end of the Cricklewood Bentley days, as the company did not acquire its own machine shop until 1929.

In the beginning, it appears that Burgess was rather keen on making a smaller car, but WO's ideas for a large touring model won the day, and that was what was drawn up at the office in Conduit Street. WO could see that any attempt to compete with established high-volume manufacturers of lower-priced cars would be doomed to failure; they had to start with low volumes and high prices, and move on from there. As he explained in his 1958 autobiography:

"The policy was a simple one. We were going to make a fast car, a good car, the best in its class; and when we had begun to show a profit and had obtained our own machine shop, then we would make a smaller, cheaper car – a bread-and-butter car in fact – as well."

So the first Bentley car would be a touring car with sporting potential, strong and reliable in all areas, and it would have a large-capacity under-stressed engine rather than a small-capacity engine which had to be revved to within an inch of its life to deliver its best performance. WO was no enthusiast of the French or Italian way of building cars, despite his success with the French DFP.

The new car was to be aimed at customers who might otherwise buy cars like the Vauxhall 30/98 or one of the larger Straker-Squires. These were very much at the top end of the market, offering strong performance from large-capacity engines, and their appeal was mainly to wealthy gentlemen with sporting interests, drawn primarily from the upper-middle classes and the aristocracy. WO had probably met many of the type among the officer class during his time serving in the military, and he no doubt believed he understood the kind of car that would appeal to them. Like him, they were "gentlemen", in the

When WO and colleagues came to design the first Bentley chassis, they sought inspiration from the most recent designs – which were those of 1914. Among the key influences was the 1914 TT Humber, not least because the man responsible for the car's design, FT Burgess, had joined the new Bentley venture. These are the Tourist Trophy Humbers, one of which Burgess himself drove, on the Isle of Man in 1914. (BDC)

While the new Bentley chassis was still in the design stages, F Gordon Crosby produced this marvellous painting that showed the car in action. As a statement of intent, it was priceless; as a reflection of what had actually been achieved, it was sheer optimism. (BDC)

style characteristic of 1920s Britain.

But as an engineer he had no real interest in building the bodywork; what he wanted to do was to design and build the chassis with its engine, gearbox and axles. The bodywork could be farmed out to specialists, as it had been with the DFP. At the end of the market at which he planned to pitch his new Bentley car, it was still standard practice for the carriage trade to provide bespoke coachwork on the chassis provided by the motor manufacturers. So the new Bentley car would be available only as a chassis, and Bentley Motors never would get involved in body manufacture – although later, as Chapter 4 explains, they would approve a range of Standard Coachwork with selected coachbuilders.

For inspiration, Bentley, Burgess and Varley studied the best sporting machines they knew about. The principles behind the designs they examined, then, were already old, although by no means outdated. There were no new post-war designs as yet; the best and most recent designs were the 1914 Grand Prix cars from Mercedes and Peugeot. Burgess of course brought with him knowledge of the 1914 TT Humbers, and Varley had a close knowledge of Vauxhall practice.

No doubt WO's railway engineering background and Burgess's experience with the TT Humbers combined to ensure that the new

Bentley frame was as strong as it could be, consistent with being light in weight. "Light" is not a word that would immediately spring to the lips of anybody looking at a Bentley chassis in the early 21st century, but the design was light by the standards of the day. In fact, *The Autocar* of 29 November 1919 described the very first Bentley as "essentially a light chassis with a very powerful engine."

There is good reason to suppose that the Bentley team may have cut corners in order to get their first prototype car on the road quickly. That first prototype shared its wheelbase of 108 inches with the 1914 Humber, and it also shared with that car the shape of its front dumb-irons. Arguably, Burgess would have stuck to what he knew best and designed them like that; equally plausible, however, is that some surplus Humber components found their way into the first Bentley. Also noticeable is the close similarity between the front axle design of the first Bentley and that of the 1914 Humber, for although the two are not exactly the same, the Humber influence is unmistakeable. Most interesting is that the 1914 Humber TT chassis had in turn been largely copied from that of the 1913 Grand Prix Peugeot. As Bentley expert Michael Hay has explained, the chassis of the first Bentley later found its way into a GP Peugeot, and the owner of that car did not realise it was not a genuine Peugeot chassis!

The spiral bevel rear axle was certainly an original design, and the semi-elliptic leaf springs on all four corners of the frame were only to be expected at that time. The Bentley team chose a cone clutch, again typical for the period, drum-type brakes on the rear wheels only (four-wheel brakes were still a few years away from popularity) and designed a sturdy four-speed gearbox with closely-spaced ratios to promote the sporting performance that was one of their design aims.

The chassis was assembled in Bentley & Bentley's DFP Service Station at New Street Mews, beginning probably some time around June or July 1919. A plaque on the wall now commemorates the birthplace of the first Bentley motor car. In charge of the assembly operation was Nobby Clarke, whom WO had met during his time in the RNAS, where Clarke had been a Chief Petty Officer; the two men had taken shelter together in a French canal when the famous Red Baron, Von Richthofen, had strafed the airfield WO was visiting in connection with his aero-engine work. Clarke would remain with Bentley Motors throughout their Cricklewood period, initially as Works Superintendent and racing manager, and later as Service Manager.

Meanwhile, work was also going ahead on the critical element of the new Bentley car – its engine. The first engine was assembled in the workshop above the DFP Service Station, in conditions of some secrecy. Those working downstairs had a pretty good idea of what was going on because they knew there was to be a new Bentley car, but they were not encouraged to take a closer look. They saw various components arriving and being carried up the stairs, but that was all.

The new engine was drawn up with a swept volume of 3 litres, and when the car was eventually introduced to the public it was actually called a Bentley 3-litre. The name seems to have caused some head-scratching when the car was first shown in public, as visitors to Olympia in 1919 were not familiar with this way of describing a car. It was certainly unusual for the time, because in Britain most cars were known by their RAC horsepower rating, which was derived from a complicated formula based on the cylinder bore diameter and which from 1921 determined how much annual tax was payable on the car. Small family cars were 6hp, 7hp and 8hp types (and among them from 1923 would be the hugely successful Austin Seven); more substantial cars for the professional classes would be 10, 12, and 14hp types; and from 16hp upwards the cars were intended for wealthy owners. Although the new Bentley engine was rated under the RAC system as a 16hp (strictly 15.9hp), it was never known as that. WO had a liking for the simplicity of metric measurements, and that probably drew him to the 3-litre name. All subsequent Bentleys built by the original company – 6½-litre, 4½-litre, 8-litre and 4-litre – would follow the same pattern, and the distinctive naming system was carried on in the 1930s after the Rolls-Royce take-over when the cars became 3½-litre and 4¼-litre models.

The new Bentley engine certainly harked back to the best Edwardian touring car designs in many ways, but it also looked forward by incorporating a number of elements seen exclusively or mainly on racing machinery. Most important, perhaps, was WO's insistence on reliability. So the engine depended on a monobloc casting –

itself not uncommon at the time – because WO knew that having a separate cylinder head placed the engine's reliability at the mercy of the sealing gasket between head and block. The crankcase was cast from aluminium, following his successful experience with the alloy in the Bentley Rotaries, the crankshaft ran in five white metal bearings, and the bearing end-caps were rigidly bolted – again for reliability.

To get the reliability he wanted – which was by no means a "given" in these relatively early days of the motor car – WO clearly envisaged an under-stressed large-capacity engine. Four cylinders would be enough. His design called for a bore of 80mm and a stroke of 149mm, the long stroke being typical of British motor car engine design of the time. The deciding factor was the motor vehicle taxation system then in force. As explained above, taxation depended on the RAC horsepower of an engine, which was calculated by a formula but depended on the bore diameter of the engine. To minimise owners' annual tax liability, British engine designers would for many years choose long strokes with narrow bores. In the case of the new Bentley engine, the long stroke involved connecting rods 295mm long, or approximately 11.5 inches between centres, and the result was an extraordinarily tall engine nearly three feet high. Early production engines had hourglass pistons with two rings, later superseded by BHB Oval pistons.

The design of the engine's top end was heavily influenced by racing practice, and in particular by the engine of the 1914 Grand Prix Mercedes. WO had had a chance to examine one of these during the war; while working on aero engines during 1915, he had assisted in its recovery from the Mercedes London showroom and its subsequent stripdown at Rolls-Royce in Derby. Like the Mercedes engine, the Bentley had a single overhead camshaft driven by bevel gears and a vertical shaft from the forward end of the crankshaft, and operating via rockers four valves per cylinder, inclined at an inclusive angle of 30 degrees. The valves were of 37mm diameter.

This four-valve arrangement had also been seen on the Grand Prix Peugeots before the war, and more detailed knowledge of these came from Clive Gallop, another of WO's wartime acquaintances (this time from the RFC) and a motor-racing mechanic before the conflict. Gallop joined the Bentley design team in the summer of 1919 and assisted in the design and

The first Bentley chassis was made into a complete car by the addition of a body that had probably been removed from a DFP chassis. This first prototype seems to have been pretty raw, but by January 1920 WO was confident enough to allow The Autocar *a test drive. This well-known photograph shows him at the wheel. The car was later rebuilt on a new production chassis.*

assembly of the first engine, but he left the company at about the same time as the first production cars were being assembled, two years later. Nevertheless, his part in the Bentley story was not yet finished, and he would again play a role in connection with the supercharged cars, as Chapter 6 explains.

Nowadays, four-valve designs are usually adopted to improve an engine's breathing, but a Bentley sales brochure would later explain that this was not the reason for the four-valve layout in the 3-litre engine. "By using two valves instead of one, the seating area is increased by 50 per cent, and in consequence the cooling surface is greater, and a greater volume of water can be circulated through the space surrounding the seatings. Further, the hammering effect on the seating of a single large valve with a strong spring is greatly diminished by using two light valves with light springs."

De-coking an engine and the attendant re-grinding of valves and their seats was a regular and necessary evil on car engines at that time, but the Bentley engine was expected to cover 20,000 miles before either became necessary.

Each cylinder also had two spark plugs for greater reliability, just as on the WO-modified DFP. The twin magnetos which fired these plugs were driven by a cross-shaft on the engine, and if one magneto failed the engine would continue to run. The water pump was gear-driven, too, as WO was no enthusiast of belt or chain drives.

The prototype engine, and a small number of subsequent experimental examples, were designed to run with a dry-sump lubrication system, and the earliest sales brochures promised this feature. However, WO was so appalled at the noise from the oil pump that he switched to a conventional wet-sump system for the production engines. These had a cast aluminium sump that was all but separate from the crankcase, so allowing maximum air flow around it to keep it cool.

A first prototype

The very first engine ran for the very first time in October 1919, on its stand in that upper-storey workshop in New Street Mews and without any form of exhaust or silencer. WO and others have relayed the story of an irate matron from a nearby hospital who came round to complain about the noise, and in deference to a supposedly dying patient the experiment was

terminated. But the engine had run: the next job was to get it installed in the chassis, and so it was lowered through a hole in the floor and bolted into the chassis waiting below in the DFP Service Station.

For the next part of the story, we have to turn to *The Other Bentley Boys* by Elizabeth Nagle and to the recollections of Leslie Pennal, who had helped assemble the car. He remembered that Clive Gallop came into the workshop after the engine had been bolted into the chassis and was "all excited to see the radiator on", adding that the car could be driven if its body were put on. "The body was standing at the side," remembered Pennal, adding that it was quickly lifted into place and held down to the chassis with some clamps. There were no seats, so a cushion was pressed into use for the driver. Gallop got behind the wheel, Pennal and another fitter, Jackson, sat on a board laid across the chassis at the back, and off they went up the mews for a test run. Amusingly, the tail of Gallop's dust-coat caught in the spinning propellor shaft and as a result he was pulled down towards the chassis before the others were able to disentangle him. When WO dropped by later to try the new car out, nobody told him that he was not the first to drive it, and Pennal remembered that he did not find out until many years afterwards.

Some accounts have suggested that the body came from the coachbuilder JH Easter (whose premises were a few doors further down the mews) or possibly Harrison's (with whom Bentley & Bentley already had a thriving relationship through their DFP business). However, probably the most likely account is that suggested by Michael Hay, who has pointed out that the body had a striking similarity to the one that Harrison's had built on one of Bentley & Bentley's DFP demonstrators. Hay also points out that it was not a very good fit – pictures clearly show a discrepancy between the line of the top of the door and its continuation on the scuttle – and all this suggests that the body had actually been removed from the DFP in order to speed up the construction of the first Bentley. The Bentley team in that London mews married it to an extra-long scuttle-panel which they made detachable to give easy access to the back of the dashboard. This was, after all, a prototype car and some teething troubles were only to be expected.

Long before the car was complete, and prob-

ably before its construction had even begun, readers of *The Autocar* had been primed about what to expect. WO had met SCH (Sammy) Davis not long after he bought his first motor cycle – Davis lived not far from the Bentley family home – and the two had met up again during the war years when Davis had been the Admiralty inspector assigned to keep an eye on WO's rotary engine work. They had become friends, and Davis had now become Sports Editor of *The Autocar*, writing under the name of Casque. So it was that the first news of what young Captain Bentley was up to appeared in that magazine's issue dated 8 March 1919. Later, in the issue dated 17 May, *The Autocar* actually carried a full specification of the new car, plus a drawing by F Gordon Crosby of what it looked like!

Crosby was a well-known automotive artist and another old friend of WO's, and his picture showed a two-seater open racing machine, clearly solidly built but featuring minimal bodywork. As WO put it himself in *The Illustrated History of the Bentley Car*: "He laid down the general line of the first bodies as soon as he got wind of what we were up to, and the reproduction of his painting which he did for us which hangs above my bed to this day was done while Burgess, Varley and I were still at the drawing stage." It was this painting which first showed the famous Bentley radiator to the world, and whether it was Crosby's own design or was produced with input from WO is an issue which remains unresolved to this day.

The first Bentley car, usually known by its chassis number of EXP1, was completed in

The very first Bentley 3-litre no longer survives, but former Technical College lecturer Alan Mallinson painstakingly recreated it in miniature over a three-year period. This exquisite 1/15th scale model is now owned by Tim Houlding. The original car was little more than a test-bed for WO's new engine, combining a chassis heavily based on that of the 1914 TT Humber with a body probably taken from a DFP.

October 1919, and Bentley Motors lost no time in getting on with the next tasks. In addition to testing and refining the new car, there was a need to arrange publicity for the new venture and to build a second chassis which might incorporate improvements learned from work on the first.

Publicity was something which WO seems to have been rather good at, and right from the start he made every effort to get his new car noticed. These efforts included obtaining a BM (Bentley Motors) registration number for it, for which he would have had to deal with the Bedfordshire licensing authority rather than the London one which registered cars in the area where Bentley Motors was based. EXP1 became BM 8287, and WO repeated the trick for the next two prototypes as well. EXP2 became BM 8752, and EXP3 became BM 9771. It all helped.

However, of more value in the longer term was to get the message out that there was (or soon would be) a new Bentley car on the market. So Bentley Motors secured a stand for the first post-war motor vehicle exhibition at London's Olympia, scheduled for November 1919. The timing was tight, and to secure a stand it was necessary to be a member of the Society of Motor Manufacturers and Traders, so Bentley Motors made use of their association with Bentley & Bentley, who of course still owned the DFP concession and had a stand already booked. Here, they displayed the post-war 12/40 model, the latest version of the car that they had developed so extensively between 1912 and 1914.

The Bentley Motors stand (number 126) was opposite the DFP stand in the main hall at Olympia and, according to AFC Hillstead in *Those Bentley Days*, was no more than "a side alley immediately below the gallery". It was, though, all they needed: there was precious little to exhibit at this stage, and the Bentley stand's proximity to the DFP stand meant that staff could keep an eye on both without too much difficulty.

Hillstead was of course the Sales Manager of Bentley & Bentley, and he and HM Bentley had already got together to draw up the first Bentley catalogue for distribution at the show. Produced by Frank Corbett, who would continue to work on Bentley sales literature for many years, it incorporated a number of pencil drawings, the expected eulogy of the planned Bentley car, and a reproduction of an F Gordon Crosby painting of the new 3-litre. Unfortunately, as Hillstead later remembered, "The small boy fraternity quickly found out that a fine coloured plate of a Bentley could be had for nothing, with the result that every copy which was lying about promptly vanished. That brought about severe rationing in

Bentley at Olympia: this is EXP3, the Harrison-bodied car which WO used as his own transport for a time and which is thought to have appeared twice on a Bentley show stand. This is probably the first appearance, in November 1920, when the stand was not actually in the main hall but at nearby White City. (Bryan Goodman)

order to reserve supplies for those people who were seriously interested in the car."

Those who were seriously interested were able to look over an exhibition chassis, which certainly looked the part but was in fact not all it appeared to be. EXP2 at this stage had not been completed, and several parts of its engine were dummied up in wood. One visitor to the stand discovered that the hard way when he tried to swing the starting-handle. From various accounts, it appears that the new Bentley – accurately described in that sales brochure as a prototype – aroused plenty of interest, but of course Bentley Motors were not yet in a position to take orders.

The next stage in the publicity process was to get the car featured in the motoring press, and to that end WO made use of his friendship with Sammy Davis at *The Autocar*. EXP1 was submitted for evaluation in January 1920 and was given appropriate coverage. Davis probably pulled a few punches: in *An Illustrated History of the Bentley Car*, WO freely acknowledged that "the noise and roughness of this machine were almost indescribable – and Sammy Davis was kind… to confine himself to 'the steady roar of the exhaust', the 'noisy' oil pump drive, and 'a peculiar penetrating grate' from 'somewhere in the engine'." Development clearly had some way to go.

During the rest of 1920, it appears that money was shuffled (in a quite legal fashion) between Bentley & Bentley and Bentley Motors in order to give the new company some working capital. Shareholders were sought, and a draft prospectus designed to attract investment and dated December 1920 shows that the company at that stage expected to build five chassis a week with a profit of £200 on each, and so to bring in a profit of around £50,000 a year. In practice, the company was already woefully short of money and made no profit in 1919, 1920 or 1921. Instead, it made a cumulative loss of £23,000 over the three years. This was not a promising start.

Although development work continued and a third chassis, EXP3, was built during 1920, there was still no real prospect of a start to production. WO had the third chassis fitted with vee-front Allweather coachwork by Harrison's in London, and took it over as his personal transport. It was almost certainly this car that was on the Bentley Motors stand at the Olympia Show in November 1920. This time, that stand (number 426) was not within the main hall but rather in the overflow section at nearby White City. Once again, there seems to have been plenty of public interest in the new car.

Some difficulties arose during the year. It appears that influential shareholders wanted Bentley Motors to contract-out the actual manufacture of their chassis and to concentrate on design work. WO was opposed to this, as well as to the suggestion that Bentley Motors should be based in the Midlands, which had already become the heart of the British motor industry. By the end of the year, he had got his way on both counts.

After an initial false start when Bentley Motors planned to buy the vast site that was RAF Tangmere near Chichester in Sussex, the company took out a mortgage on four acres of land at the junction of Oxgate Lane with the Edgware Road in Cricklewood, on the still quite rural northwest outskirts of London. This suited WO well, as he wanted to be in or near London, but it also brought more debt at a time when the company could ill afford it. Nevertheless, there seems to have been enough optimism in the air for the issue not to have been considered at all seriously. Besides, the Bentley brothers still owned the DFP concession, and not only was that bringing in a certain amount of income but it was also a valuable asset in its own right which could be sold off to raise capital at some point in the future. In practice, it would not be sold on until December 1922, by which time DFP sales were declining.

Expansion was in the air: the company still had its Registered Office at 16 Conduit Street, and in late 1920 took out a lease on a showroom at 3 Hanover Court, on Hanover Square in London W1 and close to the DFP showrooms in Hanover Street. At this stage, they had little more than an engine and a show chassis to display there, but no doubt the acquisition of a showroom felt like an important step forward.

But it was Cricklewood which would be the home of Bentley Motors throughout its existence as an independent company. The first building erected there was a large brick workshop; an army-type hut erected alongside became the new Drawing Office and accommodated Burgess, Varley and, in due course, others as well; and as the years went on and the company expanded, other buildings were erected on the site. Sadly, none of them survives today.

Bentley Motors certainly began to engage more staff, taking over a number of employees from Bentley & Bentley. Notable among these was AFC Hillstead, the Sales Manager, whom WO later described as "an excellent salesman who could drive so beautifully that he could have sold a lorry as a limousine to a duchess". Also from Bentley & Bentley came Nobby Clarke as Works Superintendent. Under him as Works Manager was Frank Clement, who had been a test engineer at Straker-Squire and now took over the management of about 10 men at Cricklewood. Arthur Saunders, later to become the foreman of the Racing Shop, joined in this period. Famous for his quick temper, he became an experienced and highly respected member of the team, whose two sons (Arthur Jr and Wally) also joined Bentley Motors. Arthur had extensive racing experience, and had been recruited by FT Burgess, for whom he had been racing and riding mechanic on the 1914 TT Humber. Fred Conway became the indispensable Stores Manager, and Leslie Pennall, another Bentley & Bentley stalwart, joined on the service side of the business.

WO always believed that he had the knack of selecting the right people to do the jobs he needed to be done, and the results certainly suggest he was right. The extraordinarily high level of devotion from the workforce both to him personally and to Bentley Motors in general is amply illustrated by the interviews in Elizabeth Nagle's book, *The Other Bentley Boys*. Yet there was no doubt, as that book also makes clear, that there was a clear division between management and workmen, between officers and troops.

This may sound strange to a modern world used to a more egalitarian system, but it was perfectly normal for Britain in the 1920s. Most of the men working at Cricklewood would also have experienced these attitudes in the armed forces during the Great War. The fact that WO himself took a keen interest both in the work being done on the shop-floor and in the welfare of his employees spoke volumes for him as a manager of people, and helped to knit the company together behind a single aim. An early Bentley employee was Joby Bowles, who told historian David Burgess-Wise how he remembered WO. (His recollections were published in Bruce H Brown's *WO Bentley and the DFP*). "He was," said Bowles, "a bit aloof and very strict, and you had to be very careful what you were doing when he was around. But he was a pleasant and fair man."

EXP 2 was the second Bentley prototype, built in 1919 and exhibited incomplete at Olympia that year. Now owned by Bentley Motors, it is today the oldest surviving Bentley in the world.

The unpainted bonnet panels were a fashion of the time, and the strap over them was as much a symbol of sporting intent as a practical measure to hold them in place at speed. Like all 3-litres built before August 1923, EXP 2 had no front brakes.

Production begins

The first "production" Bentley chassis must have been assembled over the summer of 1921, and the first customer car left the factory in August. This had chassis number 3 and was fitted with a two-seater touring body of unknown make. Chassis number 1 was held back for delivery to a more high-profile owner in September: once again, WO demonstrated his eye for publicity by ensuring that it went to wealthy playboy and motor racing enthusiast Noel Van Raalte. The Van Raalte car was bodied as a saloon by Easter, which might not have been WO's preferred choice of coachwork but was an early indication that customers were going to decide for themselves what use to make of their Bentleys. As for chassis number 2, nothing is known for certain, but there does appear to have been a chassis number 2A which was bodied as a lorry and was presumably used by Bentley Motors for collecting parts from their suppliers. There was, obviously, no point in buying a lorry built by somebody else when it was just as easy to make your own!

These early cars established the pattern that would stay with Bentleys right through the Cricklewood years. Chassis and engine numbers very rarely coincided, because assembly of the two major components proceeded at different speeds and were dependent on the delivery of supplies from different manufacturers. Chassis number 1 had engine number 3; chassis number 3 had engine number 4; and engine number 1 went into chassis number 5.

Chassis number 5 was in fact an important one

for Bentley Motors. Completed in September 1921 with what was probably a four-seat "torpedo" body by Curtis, another coachbuilder based in London's West End, it was almost certainly exhibited on the Bentley Motors stand at the November 1921 Olympia Show. With it were a special exhibition chassis (which could well have been chassis number 2) and an Allweather saloon by Harrison which was probably EXP3 making its second Olympia appearance. In fact, the Bentley Motors stand, number 162, was once again not in the main exhibition hall but in the overflow section at White City. This time, the company was able to begin taking orders. Bentley Motors was, at last, in business.

The tyres look incredibly narrow by modern standards, but are absolutely correct for the car. The two aero-screens gave some protection from flying stones, but very little else.

BM 8752

EXP 2's sporting pretensions are no better appreciated than from this angle. Though deliberately simple, in the interests of lightness, the two-seater body by Easter certainly looks the part.

Massive rear brakes were needed to stop a car capable of speeds as high as the Bentley's, especially when there were no front brakes. Note the finned drums, to aid cooling. EXP 2 would have had just one rear light when new; the two seen here were a later Road Traffic Act requirement.

The twin magnetos were mounted at the front of the engine, one on either side. Each one fired four plugs on its own side of the engine: there were eight plugs in all, with two for each of the four cylinders. This is actually a CG4 type magneto, as used from chassis number 175 onwards.

The B symbol cast into the oil filler cap was not only a maker's mark: it also allowed the cap to double as a breather. Today, though, its almost jewel-like appearance has a very special charm.

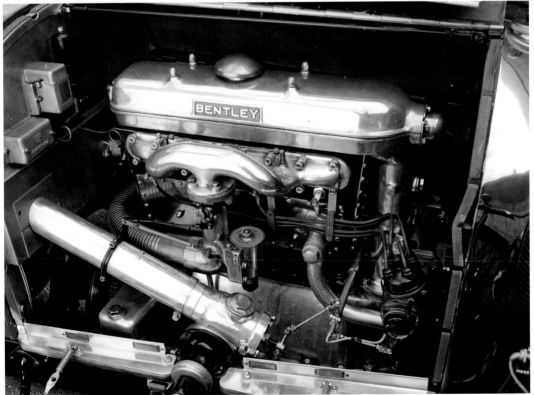

The Bentley engine had an efficient cross-flow design, and this is the exhaust side. Even the exhaust manifold seems massive, but it gave good gas-flow for maximum efficiency.

The engine currently in EXP 2 is not the original, but is nonetheless an early example dating probably from late 1922. There is a massiveness about its construction that is immediately apparent. This is the inlet side, with the single Zenith carburettor obvious in the foreground.

Built strictly as a two-seater, EXP 2 has the bare minimum of equipment necessary for high-speed motoring in the 1920s. Yet even from inside the cockpit, the car has an air of sturdiness that would become characteristic of the Bentley brand.

Clear in this picture are the splines inside the wheel hubs that slid over the axle ends. The wheels were locked in place by eared centre-caps.

The instruments and dials are redolent of boats and aircraft, but that was the fashion of the time.

The handbrake and its mechanism were massive, and were mounted outside the car in the fashion of the time in order to leave maximum room inside. The drilled holes were not for effect, but to reduce weight.

The radiator proudly carries a winged-B motif, with the background to the letter in blue enamel, now somewhat faded. Above it is a temperature gauge, which warned the driver of overheating – as long as he or she could see it from the driving seat!

Chapter Two

The Early 3-Litres

1921-1924

As Bentley Motors quickly found out, there was still a long way to go before they could legitimately call themselves car manufacturers. Having designed a car that not only worked but worked well was only the beginning: getting it into production was a very different matter. This aspect of motor manufacture may well have been something that WO had simply not looked into because it did not interest him: after all, one of the problems that Gwynne's had found when he was working on aero engines for them was that his ideas were good but that he expected somebody else to sort out the production implications for him.

Once the demands of manufacturing entered the picture, costs began to escalate. It was clear from a very early stage that Bentley Motors would not be able to make components for the new car themselves, and that these would have to be bought in. It was Burgess who made the arrangements with manufacturing companies, and as he did so, costs began to accumulate quite alarmingly. Bentley Motors had estimated in January 1919 that they would be able to offer their chassis for £750, of which £200 would be clear profit. In order to maintain that clear profit of £200, the figure they had used to entice investors, Burgess calculated in September 1920 that they would need to charge £1150, no less than £400 more than intended, for the completed chassis.

One problem was that parts would have to be bought in from a wide variety of manufacturers located all over the country. Chassis frames, for example, were to come from Mechans in Glasgow; Cosmos Engineering in Bristol supplied many items (and in due course relinquished Peter Purves from their staff to become Bentley's Chief Buyer). Sterling Metals in Coventry cast the engine blocks, the cam casings and covers, and the gearbox casings. ENV in Birmingham made most of the gears, and probably all of them.

Burgess had planned for a large number of other items to come from a firm in Coventry, and Bentley Motors were fortunate that WO discovered a company nearer to Cricklewood who were looking for business and were only too pleased to take on the work for Bentley. This was the Automotive Engineering Company of Twickenham, who had been engaged on war work and whose contracts had now dried up; in the end, WO estimated that in the early days they supplied about 80% of every Bentley car.

It was potentially a logistical nightmare, but Bentley Motors were fortunate in having staff who were able to keep a firm control of what was happening. Key among these was Fred Conway, usually known only by his surname, who ran the stores at Cricklewood. Even so, WO noted rather wistfully in *The Cars in my Life*, by 1922, "we had become not manufacturers of motor cars as we had intended, but assemblers and testers, and that remained our function almost until the end." Another severe hindrance of which he complained, this time in

An Illustrated History of the Bentley Car, was the lack of a machine shop:

"We had to put out all our machining... we desperately lacked any kind of flexibility or even independence. We were, in fact, strictly in our suppliers' hands. We had to give our orders a long time ahead, and then could neither reduce nor increase them according to our ever-changing needs." Not until 1929 – by which date the 3-litre had run its course – did Bentley Motors get its own machine shop at Cricklewood. It made a big difference to production, but that difference came too late to save the company.

By the time the 3-litre Bentley entered production in the late summer of 1921, the design of the chassis frame had standardised on a wheelbase of 117.5 inches, more commonly expressed in Bentley literature as 9ft 9½in. It was of course a ladder-frame design of chassis, with two sturdy steel side-members braced by four substantial cross-members and by tubular tie-rods at front and rear. All the frame components were made from 9-gauge (0.144in thick) steel, and Mechans assembled them with rivets at their Glasgow factory before shipping them to Cricklewood. Here, the first job was to drill mounting holes for other components, and this was done by laying each frame out on the workshop floor and marking it up with the aid of lengths of wire.

Not only was the wheelbase five inches longer than it had been on the first prototype cars, but the design of the front dumb-irons had also been changed, and these now had a more gradual downward curve. The probable reason was that this flatter shape reduced the stresses in this area of the chassis frame. The 11-gallon fuel tank was normally mounted at the rear (although on some competition cars, such as those built for the 1922 TT, a larger tank would be fitted amidships to improve weight distribution). Semi-elliptic leaf springs provided the suspension, as they did on almost every car of the time, and there was a safety stop behind the rear brackets of the front pair to prevent the axle moving backwards if a main leaf failed. Damping was by DN friction dampers, which could be adjusted by simply clamping the friction discs more tightly together.

The front springs were mounted above the axle, but the rear springs were mounted underneath the axle to control torque reaction more effectively when the drive was taken up. The front axle was a simple beam type, now without the dipped centre of the prototype, which had probably been inspired by the Humber TT design. It had a boss at each end, and through each boss was a swivel pin on which was mounted the steering stub axle. There was an adjustable track rod between the stub axles and of course a drop-arm from the worm-and-wheel steering box. The steering column was designed for easy adjustment of its rake to suit different styles of bodywork.

The rear axle was of necessity a more complicated assembly, and in the beginning was built up from two steel pressings (supplied by a company called Barnes) that were welded together. The banjo casing for the differential came from Rubery Owen at Darlaston in the West Midlands, and the gears for the spiral bevel and pinion final drive were machined by ENV in Birmingham. Half-shafts came from yet another supplier, with splines at the inboard ends but bearings at the outer ends to give a semi-floating arrangement. There was a removable differential nose-piece

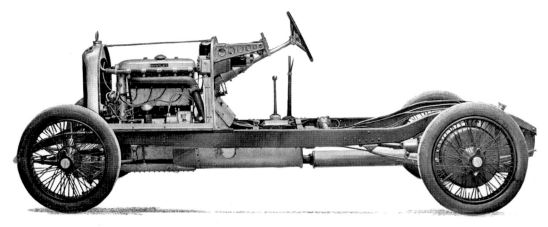

This was the early 3-litre chassis, as sales catalogues showed it to prospective buyers. Bodywork was not Bentley Motors' concern – although, as Chapter 4 shows – it soon did become a matter of concern. Note the lack of front-wheel brakes on this 1921 example.

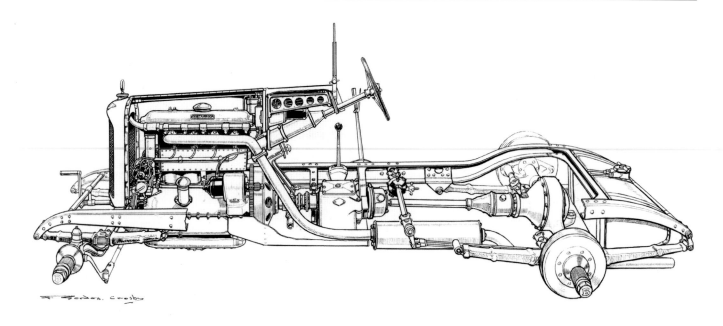

F Gordon Crosby produced this magnificent schematic drawing of a 3-litre for The Autocar. *This is of course the original 9ft 9½-inch wheelbase chassis, again with brakes on the rear wheels only.*

to simplify access for maintenance.

All these elements came together in a designated area of the Bentley works at Cricklewood, the Axle Shop. Brakes were also fitted here, and on the early cars these were on the rear wheels only. They were large ribbed drum types of 400mm diameter with aluminium shoes, actuated mechanically via rods from the pedal or the handbrake (mounted outboard of the driver and therefore almost invariably also outside the bodywork). At this period, the relative positions of the three pedals had not become standardised, and the Bentley brake pedal was on the right with the accelerator in the middle between it and the clutch. A balance beam differential provided side-to-side compensation to give even braking.

The road wheels were 21-inch wire-spoked types manufactured by Rudge Whitworth in Coventry, "the only item in the make-up of the cars that was stock standard and not specially made for us," according to WO in *An Illustrated History of the Bentley Car.* Their hubs were secured to the axle ends by tapered splines and a key, plus a locking ring in the shape of an eared hubcap. As on all cars of the time, it was advisable to check them regularly for loose or broken spokes – although squeaks and rattles usually gave these problems away if a visual inspection had not – and sensible owners removed them once in a while to prevent them rusting onto their splines.

Right from the start, the plan had been to give

the new Bentley car a gearbox with four forward speeds plus reverse. These were the days before synchromesh, and this was a "crash" gearbox which demanded that a driver learn how to double-declutch in order not to grate the gears. The gearbox had been designed in-house and the first A-type boxes were distinguished by six securing nuts on their top covers. The very first examples had no speedometer drive (the speedometer was driven by a pulley arrangement on the propeller shaft), but a drive take-off was soon fitted to the front of the box. The whole assembly was mounted on three points within the chassis frame, the front mounting being adjustable for height.

Drive reached the gearbox, which was not in unit with the engine, through a cone-type clutch and was transferred to the rear axle by a propeller shaft with a "plunging" or "pot" joint. This depended on phosphor-bronze sliding blocks and pads to take up variations in the distance between the gearbox output shaft and the differential nose-piece caused by the movement of the rear axle.

The engine realistically developed about 69bhp at 3500rpm on a compression ratio of 4.3:1. It was of essentially the same design as the prototype that had first run in October 1919, but there had been a number of quite major changes. Appalled by the noise from the oil scavenger pump located under the dashboard, WO had insisted that the dry-sump lubrication system should be changed for a more conventional wet-sump type. However, to ensure adequate cooling, he had had the new sump drawn up as an almost separate casting from the crankcase, the design allowing cool air to pass below the crankcase and over the top of the sump.

The valve actuation arrangements had also been changed. The camshaft now rotated in the opposite direction and had three cams per cylinder rather than the two of the prototype engine, two operating the inlet valves through a pair of rockers, and the third operating the exhaust valves through a single forked rocker. Ignition reliability had been improved by using twin ML G4 magnetos instead of the prototype's single Bosch unit; these were arranged to fire the spark plugs in a given cylinder simultaneously to give the maximum spark for combustion. If only one magneto was working, only one of each cylinder's two plugs would fire, but the engine would still run. The magnetos were driven directly from a cross-shaft at the front of the engine, and the water pump was now driven by skew gears instead of from this cross-shaft. The carburettor, too, had been changed from the Claudel Hobson CZP, which had been readily available when the first engine

was being built, to a five-jet Smith 45VS type. There was an external high-pressure oil filter mounted on the left side of the crankcase.

The electrical system was supplied by Smith's and centred on a 12-volt battery, charged by a dynamo mounted on the bulkhead and driven directly off the rear end of the camshaft via fabric universal joints. There was also an electro-magnetic cut-out box which automatically connected the dynamo to the battery once it was spinning fast enough to generate charge, and which broke the connection when the dynamo speed dropped below charging levels so that the battery did not discharge back through the dynamo. To prevent the battery from becoming over-charged on long runs, a switch on the dash allowed the driver to put the dynamo out of circuit.

Among the final elements of the car to be fitted were the instruments, the radiator shell and the bonnet panels. Dashboards varied widely from car to car, and were more or less built to customer choice; the cast metal bulkheads on which they were mounted also varied to suit the chosen bodywork. Open cars typically had dashboards with an Elektron (turned

The 1921 Show chassis in the workshop at Cricklewood. It has been suitably bulled-up for its duties. Chassis were supplied with bonnet panels, but of course they were removed in this case to show the engine

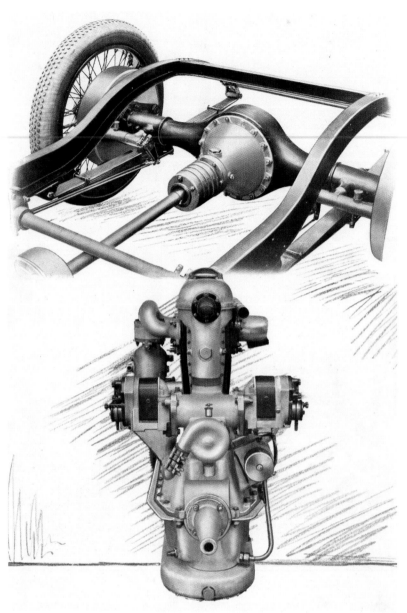

years – and even WO himself – to refer to "Blue Label" cars. As for the bonnet panels, these would be made to suit the individual chassis, the position and height of the bulkhead having been arranged to suit the body style that the customer had ordered. Bentley Motors subcontracted the job of fitting bonnet panels to Ewart & Sons, who would send a fitter round to do the job. Ewarts were based in Camden Town, a few miles nearer the centre of London than Cricklewood. They also built some complete bodies on Bentley chassis, including the special racing bodies for the 1922 TT cars.

Once a Bentley chassis had been completed in the Erecting Shop, it would pass to the Running Shop, where static tests would be carried out and the chassis would be prepared for road test. This meant securing a box filled with concrete to the rear of the chassis to simulate the weight of the completed body. Chassis would then go out on test, usually driven by Bob Tomlins, the chief road tester. After any necessary adjustments had been made, they would be signed off for delivery to the coachbuilder. Construction of each body would take anywhere between three and six months (a substantial part of this time was used up waiting for the paint to dry), and the completed cars then returned to Cricklewood, where they would be given another thorough inspection to check whether the new bodywork was causing any problems – and indeed it was not uncommon for cars to be returned to the coachbuilder for rectification work. Only when the completed car had satisfied the Bentley inspection was it given its five-year guarantee and delivered to the customer.

Like all the Bentley models that followed it from the Cricklewood factory, the 3-litre was essentially a low-volume, hand-made product. As a result, it is very likely that no two cars were ever exactly the same even before they left Cricklewood to be bodied.

This kind of variation is endemic to hand-made cars. At Cricklewood, there would have been a constant process of evolution in the assembly shop. This would have taken two forms. First came the planned development, in which part of the design was changed to bring about an improvement. This is most obvious in such things as changes of thickness in the metal of the 3-litre's chassis frame.

But this kind of planned development was

Buyers were expected to take an interest in the engineering details; after all, Bentley Motors were not supplying the bodywork. The rear axle and differential are seen here, together with a head-on view of the engine with its twin magnetos and, in this 1921 illustration, a single Smith carburettor.

or machined) finish, while closed cars more commonly had a wooden dashboard. Instruments included a speedometer, a rev counter in more overtly sporting models, sometimes a clock, sometimes an air pressure gauge for the fuel system (which worked by vacuum), and of course a master switchbox. Most instruments were made by Smith's, although speedometers also came from Jaeger.

The Bentley radiator shell was made of nickel silver (usually described then as German silver) and bore the winged B symbol of the marque. On early cars these badges all had a blue enamelled background, which led enthusiasts in later

probably quite often subverted by unplanned circumstances. For example, the changeover from the original pan-type engine sump to the later "big sump" was in theory made at chassis number PH1454 in 1927. However, there are several later cars which seem to have had the early sump from new. What probably happened was a temporary shortage of the new sumps, caused for example by a delay in deliveries from the manufacturer. To avoid holding up production, some spare sumps of the old design would have been taken from the spares kept in the stores and used in production until supplies of the new design became available again.

These variations between one 3-litre chassis and the next would have been supplemented by many others. There would, for example, have been times when one of the fitters might have found a new and more satisfactory way of attaching an item to the chassis than had been used before. This would then perhaps be adopted as standard. We also know one of the checks made when a newly-bodied car returned to Cricklewood from the coachbuilder was to ensure that the road springs were suitable for the weight of the body; in cases where they were not, the Cricklewood staff changed them for a more suitable type. Though driven by practical necessity, these changes introduced yet more individual variation.

One final point is well worth making. Bentley Motors sanctioned cars to be built in batches, initially of six and later of 25. At any one time, several chassis would be under construction in the Erecting Shop at Cricklewood, and the teams working on them would be making progress at slightly different rates. So chassis were not necessarily completed in numerical order. Equally, the engines were built separately and were fitted into the chassis as they were completed. As a result, matching chassis and engine numbers in a Cricklewood Bentley occurred only extremely rarely.

1921-1922 – the first production cars

It was *The Autocar* that carried the big announcement in its issue of 27 August 1921. "Bentley Cars in Production," ran the banner headline, followed in smaller type by "First cars to be delivered shortly". Somewhat prophetically, in view of Bentley Motors' constant money troubles over the next few years, the article went on to say that "throughout operations,

The 3-litre engine. The transversely mounted magnetos, driven by a cross shaft off the camshaft drive, are easily accessible, as are the oil filter, oil filler and starter.

finance has been a handicap" – although it did balance that remark by adding "as it also has been a handicap to practically every firm". These were not yet easy times for the British motor industry.

In fact, *The Autocar* was a little late with its announcement because the first production Bentley car had been delivered to its new owner on 3 August, more than three weeks earlier. Its

Some customers bought their 3-litres specifically for competition use. This remarkable two-seater dates from 1922 and belonged to GA Eggerton, who is presumably in the driving seat. The picture was taken at Brooklands, on the famous banking.

chassis must have been built up during July 1921, and build may actually have started even earlier than that. Numerically, however, the chassis of the open two-seater that was delivered to Ivor Llewellyn at the start of August was not the first production Bentley; it was actually number 3.

That Mr Llewellyn should have been the first customer to take delivery was more by accident than design. WO had allocated chassis number 1 to a man who was in the public eye because

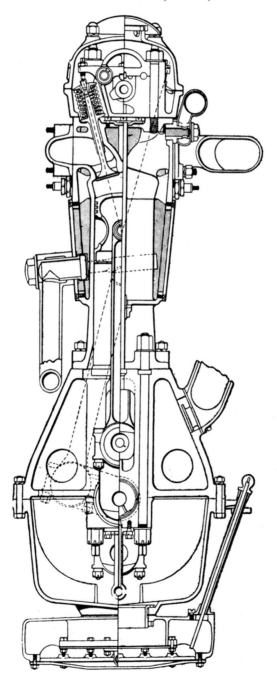

Section through the 3-litre engine gives a clear impression of how slim and tall the design was.

he knew that this individual would get the car noticed and attract attention to the new marque. However, the body for chassis number 1, a rather rakish-looking closed coupé, must have taken longer to build than the relatively simple open two-seater that Mr Llewellyn had ordered for his car. Determined nevertheless to make the most out of the delivery of chassis number 1, WO therefore probably delayed telling his colleagues at *The Autocar* until the car was well on the way to completion. (It is not clear who built the body for chassis number 3. The car still exists, in the USA, but Bentley number 1 was last heard of in 1931.)

In view of WO's vision of the Bentley as a chassis for lightweight, open bodywork, there was some irony about the fact that the customer for chassis number 1 had ordered closed bodywork. Noel Van Raalte was a wealthy Cambridge-educated socialite and playboy, a well-known figure within the motor racing fraternity and a major backer of the KLG spark plug company. He was also a friend of WO's, and he was in many ways the ideal person to promote the new marque within the social circles where Bentley Motors hoped to find most of their customers.

The car was delivered in September 1921, and Van Raalte almost immediately began to spread the word about his high opinion of it. Before the end of the month he had written to the Editor of *The Autocar* magazine, who published his letter in the issue dated 1 October. "The reason I bought a Bentley," wrote Van Raalte, "was because of its exceptional performance in all respects on the road". He went on to point out that he had owned two Rolls-Royce cars and was an admirer of the marque, but that he thought the Bentley was actually better – on top of which it cost £750 less.

Ironically, perhaps, chassis number 1 was not fitted with open sporting coachwork of the type WO had in mind, but rather with a rakish-looking closed coupé body. Opinions differ as to who constructed it, but Michael Hay believes it was built by JH Easter, who were of course Bentley Motors' landlords in New Street Mews and had their own body-building business further along the same mews. One way or another, that closed body must have added no more than around 5½cwt (280kg) to the total weight of the car in order to be granted the five-year Bentley guarantee.

Close to WO's idea of what the 3-litre was all about was the car that later became a demonstrator for Bentley Motors' Sales manager, AFC Hillstead. Completed in September 1921, and doubtless under construction at the same time as the Llewellyn and Van Raalte cars, this actually had chassis number 5 and engine number 1. The car was originally bodied as a four-seater by JH Easter, but then passed to FW Burgess for experimental (ie development) work. It was then rebodied as a sporty-looking two-seater by Ewart & Son Ltd at the same time as the bodies for the three 1922 TT cars and to the same design. The spare wheel was mounted horizontally under the tail, where it protruded from the rounded rump of the body. This was a very striking-looking car, with its aluminium bodywork scratched and then varnished to give an iridescent white effect, and contrasting red wings. It certainly gave a good idea of what a sporting Bentley could look like.

Production got under way quite slowly at first, as was only to be expected. Somewhere around 22 chassis had been built by the end of 1921, which meant that 3-litres were being completed at a rate of around five a month. That delay between completion of a chassis and its return to Cricklewood with its new body for a final check-over meant that the typical customer might therefore have had to wait around four or five months from placing an order to actual delivery. Many customers were in fact fitting the lightweight, sporting bodywork that WO had always imagined would suit his chassis, but fashions were already beginning to change and there was a slow but increasing demand right across the motor trade for All-weather and closed bodies. This trend would in due course have its effect on the 3-litre.

Meanwhile, Bentley Motors were of course still trying their utmost to get the word about their new car out to the ears of those who were its most likely customers. Placing cars with customers who would be likely to influence the opinions of their peers, as had occurred with Noel Van Raalte, was just one way of doing this. More effective still was likely to be participation in motor racing.

As Chapter 8 shows, motor racing mattered as Britain entered the 1920s. It was the most effective way of generating publicity for a car, and there was no doubt that it had a particular appeal to the wealthy, leisured clientele that

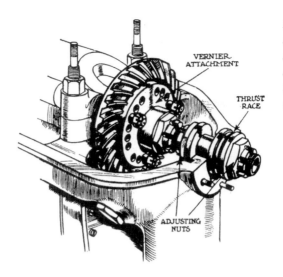

Detail of the camshaft drive bevel, which is attached to its shaft by a vernier and adjusted by means of the two nuts shown.

Bentley Motors wanted to attract. WO himself had seen how effective it could be from his pre-war experience with the DFP car, and on top of that he was a motor racing enthusiast himself. So from a very early stage, there were plans to get Bentleys into competition.

The cars had already been seen in competition earlier in 1921, and Frank Clement's win in the sprint race at Brooklands had already begun to arouse interest in the Bentley marque. But that car had been a prototype: what WO needed to demonstrate was that his production cars were capable of winning races with only minimal modifications.

The decision seems to have been taken in November 1921. Bentley Motors would run what was in effect a racing programme with the specific intention of attracting publicity. There would be an entry in the Indianapolis 500 at the end of May 1922, and a further entry in the Isle of Man Tourist Trophy in June. Whether the aim of entering the Indianapolis race was to attract wealthy American customers is not clear; it could well have been. The TT entry, however, was more readily understandable, not least because WO himself had already driven the Isle of Man course as a competitor.

So four chassis – one for Indianapolis and three for the TT – were allocated to the Experimental Shop in January 1922, where Frank Clement began their preparation. The scale of this undertaking can hardly be under-estimated: the four racing machines represented the best part of a month's production at the time. Nevertheless, the value of the racing effort can also not be under-estimated. While the Indianapolis entry is probably best described as a brave effort, the TT race did the Bentley reputation a power of good. The cars finished in second, fourth and fifth places and were the only complete three-car team to finish the race. Sales Manager AFC Hillstead records in his book, *Those Bentley Days*, that the TT success attracted an enthusiastic dealer to sign up as the company's Lancashire representative on the spot. "For all practical purposes," reported the *Sunday Times* of 25 June, "they were standard stock cars as sold to the general public". That was exactly the sort of publicity that WO wanted.

There are more details of the Bentley TT entry in Chapter 8, but the important result as far as the company was concerned was that the TT success also led to a demand for "TT replicas". So Bentley Motors obliged, delivering more than 70 examples between late 1922 and 1924. That kind of response really mattered: it represented about six months' chassis production for Bentley Motors at the time.

If WO and his colleagues had looked back over their first year in business, they could have believed that they had made a good start. They had built around 150 chassis. Of these, 144 had been completed and delivered to customers, and the others were still being completed by coachbuilders. They had attracted new custom and gathered valuable acclaim for the marque through successes at Brooklands and in the Isle of Man TT. And there had been no problems that suggested the new design was wide of the mark. There had indeed been a problem early on when customers had reported gearboxes jumping out of third gear, but this had been swiftly traced to selector forks that were bending. FT Burgess had redesigned the forks, and the problem did not recur.

1922-1923 – TT Replicas and a longer wheelbase

With the best part of a year's sales experience under their belts, Bentley Motors no doubt

Dating from November 1923, this is Speed Model chassis 415, with an unidentified body featuring extravagantly flared wings, photographed in Devon in December 1924 while competing in the London-Exeter-London Trial.

began to wonder what new features they could offer for the 1923 season – which, illogically but traditionally within the motor trade, would begin in the autumn of 1922. Not that there was anything fundamentally wrong with the existing 3-litre chassis; quite the contrary. However, something new was needed for the simple reason that novelty attracts publicity and publicity attracts sales.

One thing that had become very clear during those first 12 months was that not every customer was going to fit a lightweight open touring body to the Bentley chassis. We know from surviving records that many cars were fitted with All-weather bodies, many of them with four seats. Although open cars were still the norm in the early 1920s, the fashion was already changing as customers began to recognise the benefits of at least some form of weather protection.

This drift towards four-seater bodies helped to highlight a shortcoming of the original Bentley chassis. This was that the 9ft 9½-inch wheelbase did not provide enough room for coachbuilders to create four-seater bodies with rear legroom of the sort that their clients generally wanted. Whether this was really a hindrance to sales is impossible to say, but Bentley Motors must have realised that the option of a longer chassis would give their product more appeal.

As a result, for 1923 an alternative wheelbase of 130 inches (usually known as the 10ft 10in chassis) became available. It weighed around 56lb (25kg) more than the original chassis, which remained available. In addition to longer side-members, the long-wheelbase chassis was fitted with locomotive-type strut gear underneath the side rails for additional strength. Perhaps this was WO's railway experience coming to the fore. The first of the new long-wheelbase models had chassis number 161 and was actually delivered with a Harrison saloon body in December 1922.

Notable was that the Bentley guarantee now allowed for much heavier bodies than before: the 1922-season 3-litre had been designed for an overall weight of 25-26cwt (1270-1320kg) but the maximum permissible weight was now 35cwt (1778kg). Changes to the camshaft and carburation of the 3-litre engine made at about this time may be evidence of an attempt to compensate for this extra weight. The new BM2391 camshaft replaced the original BM1800

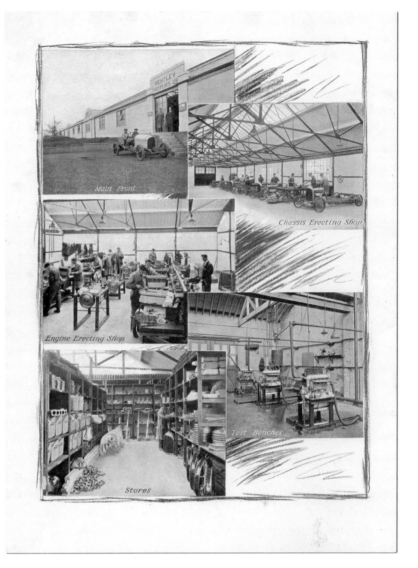

type, while Bentley's own modification of the five-jet Smith carburettor now became standard, and took on the name of Smith-Bentley 45BVS.

Even so, customers had to accept that no more than around 70mph would be available with heavy bodywork when the short-wheelbase car with touring body could achieve more than 80mph. If that sounds like a significant compromise, it is important to remember that these were the early 1920s, when 70mph from any car was something to be admired, let alone from one with a full-sized saloon body.

However, customers who bought heavy bodywork for their long-wheelbase 3-litre chassis did not have to suffer setbacks in every department. To counter the additional weight, Bentley fitted a lower-geared back axle and provided lower gearing in the intermediate ratios of the

Views of Cricklewood: this montage of pictures from the earliest days shows (clockwise from top) a chassis about to go out on test; the Chassis Erecting Shop; the Engine Test Shop; the Stores; and the Engine Erecting Shop.

gearbox, which in this application was known as the B type. It had a slightly narrower gate than the A type gearbox, which continued to be fitted to the short-chassis cars.

Bentley's offerings for the 1923 season were of course also enhanced by the TT Replica cars, of which the first examples were delivered towards the end of 1922. To call them TT Replicas was perhaps stretching credibility a little, because they were very different indeed from the cars that had performed so well in the TT race in June 1922. What they did have was the high-compression (5.3:1) engine of the TT cars, a special set of gear ratios, a tall 3.43:1 final drive and Hartford dampers. Most had the standard-issue five-jet Smith carburettor, but Bentley Motors did offer the option of replacing this by a Claudel Hobson CZP type. What they did not have was the spartan two-seat racing bodies that Ewart & Sons had constructed for the team cars, the special flat radiators which had been designed to get extra speed, or the additional 22-gallon fuel tank mounted amidships.

Nevertheless, they did offer customers the exclusivity that is always associated with a limited-edition model, and they did deliver better performance than the standard cars. Most of them seem to have had lightweight four-seater open bodies by Vanden Plas, which would have made the most of their extra performance. Most of them must also have had the CG4 magnetos which replaced the original G4 type on all 3-litres towards the end of 1922; the first chassis to have that was number 175. No doubt WO himself saw the TT Replicas as something close to the embodiment of his early dreams for the Bentley motor car.

In terms of sales, the 1923 season showed a valuable improvement over Bentley Motors' first full year of trading. A total of 204 chassis had been delivered, and there were of course others out at coachbuilders awaiting completion. The new 10ft 10in chassis had been a major success, and had accounted for nearly half the total cars delivered; it had also sold more than twice as many as the standard-wheelbase chassis. In due course, the long chassis would go on to become the most numerous variant of the 3-litre, accounting for around half of all those built in the eight years of production between 1921 and 1929.

Nevertheless, there was still a strong demand for the older chassis length. If the totals of standard-wheelbase and TT replica cars were added together, the 9ft 9½-inch wheelbase still came out just ahead on numbers. Generally speaking, those who wanted maximum performance had ordered light, open bodies on the short wheelbase while those who wanted grander or closed bodies had gone for the long wheelbase. However, there had inevitably been exceptions to this rule of thumb: customers never behave predictably!

1923-1924 – four-wheel brakes and the Speed Model

For the 1924 season, the Bentley range underwent what we might now think of as a realignment. First, as already indicated, the 10ft 10in wheelbase became standard, leaving the original 9ft 9½in wheelbase as the more sporting option. The short chassis was then also offered in a special high-performance version that was marketed as the Speed Model and in effect replaced the TT Replica.

These changes demanded others elsewhere in the specification. All the cars up to this point had managed with brakes on the rear wheels only, and indeed most other cars of the early 1920s did the same. However, the additional weight associated with the long-wheelbase chassis and the additional performance associated with the Speed Model must together have been enough to persuade WO that his cars needed brakes on the front wheels as well.

Some writers have suggested that his own experience as a driver of one of the team cars in the June 1922 TT race persuaded WO that his cars needed brakes on all four wheels and not just on the rear pair. This may also be correct, even if the time lapse of more than a year before the new brakes entered production seems rather long. However, WO would also have known that the DFP, which Bentley & Bentley were still importing, had boasted four-wheel brakes since autumn 1921. He must have known enough about work going on elsewhere in the motor industry to have recognised that such a development was inevitable. In such circumstances it was certainly better for the Bentley to be a leader in its field rather than to have to play a rather undignified game of catch-up.

So the 1924-season cars were all fitted with four-wheel brakes. In due course, owners of existing 3-litres were offered the option of upgrading their cars to the new standard for extra cost, and these upgrades would mostly have been carried out when the cars came in for service or other attention. Probably the majority of cars were modified. Like those already on the rear wheels, the front brakes were large drums designed by Bentley and using the French Perrot principles. Rod operation, still almost universal in the motoring world, was employed on all models. Although the company had initially experimented with hydraulic brakes on EXP2, they had trouble with leaks, and hydraulic brakes were never used on any production Bentley from Cricklewood. It was FT Burgess who designed the production four-wheel braking installation, which came with a redesigned front axle and some modifications to the steering. There was also a single adjuster under the floor which enabled the wear on all four brakes to be taken up simultaneously.

The four-wheel brakes were announced to the public in *The Autocar* of 21 September 1923, but they had certainly been fitted to some cars before that. Among the first to have them would have been the early examples of the new Speed Model. The final specification for this was signed off by WO in July 1923 and the first chassis, number 356, was put on show in Bentley's showrooms in Hanover Street, W1 after its completion that August.

Such was the reputation of the Bentley by this time that several famous sporting motorists of the period made their bids to buy the first of the new high-performance models. However, no doubt Bentley Motors made their selection from the prospective buyers carefully, and the chassis eventually went to the surgeon Dr AH Rabagliati, one of WO's close friends. It was fitted with a four-seat tourer body by Cadogan before being shipped to the doctor's home in Durban, South Africa.

Key to the Speed Model was a high-performance derivative of the 3-litre engine which shared its 5.3:1 compression ratio with the engine in the TT Replicas; the standard engines still ran at 4.3:1. The earliest cars had a single Smith five-jet carburettor, but work was being done at Cricklewood to get more power out of the engine and the specification changed just over a year later. In place of the standard 4.23:1 final drive, a taller 3.785:1 axle could be fitted to improve maximum speed, with a 3.923:1 option also available if a customer insisted on fitting heavy bodywork. The Speed Model chassis also had Hartford dampers, as had been fitted to the earlier TT Replica types.

A distinguishing feature of the Speed Model chassis was a red enamel background to the winged-B radiator badge in place of the blue background used on other 3-litres. However, the so-called "Red Label" was never seen at Cricklewood as an essential or exclusive characteristic of the Speed Models. If a customer wanted a red badge on his ordinary 3-litre, no doubt he only had to say the word.

For the 1924 season, there were also some running changes to the engine. The early four-bolt rocker cover gave way to a six-bolt type which now had no breather, and there were new drive arrangements for the dynamo, which had originally been driven off the back of the camshaft by a geared-up drive that increased its running speed. On the 1924 cars, a direct drive was employed.

Chassis sales for the 1924 season showed a further increase, with a grand total of 402. This figure was approaching three times the total chassis sold in the company's first year of trading, so there was every reason on a superficial level to believe that the business was heading in the right direction. This time, the lion's share was taken by the long-wheelbase chassis with 266 deliveries. There had been just two standard short-chassis cars, plus four TT Replicas and a very healthy 130 Speed Models on the short chassis.

This success had been achieved in spite of the loss of a number of chassis that were destroyed or damaged in a fire at the coachbuilder Gurney Nutting in Croydon on Good Friday, 18 April 1924. Research by Tom Clarke and Jack Triplett has revealed that 13 Bentley chassis and seven

This was perhaps the "sensible" approach to bodywork on the 3-litre chassis. It is an All-weather type by Arnold, on chassis number 444 from January 1924. The fabric roof folded down but left windows and frames in place to provide protection from draughts. All-weathers gradually gave way to closed saloons as the 1920s wore on.

The long chassis with its 10ft 10in wheelbase was introduced for 1923, and the four-seat tourer body on this one emphasises that extra length to good effect. The car is on chassis 180, and was delivered in February 1923.

Owned by Andy Hall, it carries a body by the London firm of Connaught. Note how there are two doors on the left-hand side but only one on the right. Handbrake and gear lever made sure there was no door next to the driver, who would get into the car on the kerb side. The amber turn indicator at the base of the windscreen support is obviously a modern addition.

of other makes were affected; one or more of the Bentleys had been intended for the British Empire Exhibition at Wembley that month. It appears that at least two of the Bentley chassis were salvaged and rebuilt, and parts of one became the works breakdown truck, but Gurney Nutting was out of action until August 1924, when the company re-opened in new premises in Chelsea. Michael Hay's researches have revealed that some parts of the other fire-damaged chassis found their way into the hands of certain less scrupulous members of the motor trade and were built into cars that were then passed off as Bentleys. One of these ended up

The Connaught tourer body looks even more attractive with its hood up. Without side screens in place, however, weather protection for the occupants was minimal.

in the hands of the celebrated conductor Sir Thomas Beecham.

It was now very clear that there were two distinct groups of buyers for Bentley chassis: one wanted a reliable high-performance chassis as the basis of a prestigious saloon car, while the other wanted the same mechanical elements in a shorter chassis that would be fitted with lighter sporting bodywork. For the first group, WO had already begun to think in terms of an even more powerful machine, which in due course would materialise as the 6½-litre six-cylinder Bentley.

But the 1924 season also marked a turning-point of a different kind in the fortunes of Bentley Motors. In June 1923, right at the end of the 1923 season, a Bentley had been entered for the new Le Mans 24-hour race in France and had come home in a highly creditable fourth place. Things would never be quite the same again, either for the company or for its customers.

Immediately noticeable in a comparison of this front view with that of EXP 2 (see page 23) are the friction dampers. This car has also been fitted with four-wheel brakes, which did not reach production until August 1923. Most owners had their cars upgraded when the new brakes became available.

Position of power! The dashboard was entirely functional, and customers expected no more, but there was never a standard design. The large brass plaque in the centre records the car's chassis and engine numbers, and is a later addition by an understandably proud owner. The cylindrical object above the passenger side screen is the motor for the link-driven windscreen wipers.

The 3-litre speedometer read to 100mph. It was labelled not only with the Bentley name but also with the chassis type.

The switchbox, on the right here, carried the car's chassis number. Note also the advance and retard levers around the steering wheel boss, and the drilled pedals – intended to reduce weight but copied on more modern cars as a stylistic feature.

The fuel tank was always at the back of the chassis. The profusion of lights would not have been on the car when it was new, but do enable it to take to the roads with some safety today.

The extra length of the 10ft 10in chassis was put to good use in providing leg-room for the rear-seat passengers. Just visible here is part of the wooden body frame, which forms the upright against which the door shuts.

The famous Blue Label. A larger badge with blue enamelled background was used on six-cylinder cars.

The monogrammed step has a period charm today, but was strictly functional, easing entry and exit for rear-seat passengers on the offside. As there were two doors on the nearside, there was a longer running-board there.

Bearing the scars of nearly 90 years of life, this engine is nevertheless the one that was fitted when the car was new, and proudly still displays its original identification number on the starter motor housing formed by the left-hand engine bearer.

The twin magnetos were driven from a cross-shaft at the front of the engine.

A comparison of this engine with the one in EXP 2 (see page 23) reveals some changes. There are now six bolts on the top cover rather than four. As built, this car would have had a single Smith-Bentley five-jet carburettor, but at some stage it has been fitted with the twin SU G5 "sloper" carburettors which gave more power for the 1925 season.

The fuel delivery system on this car is far more
elaborate than that on EXP 2.

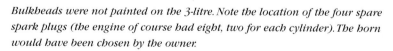

Bulkheads were not painted on the 3-litre. Note the location of the four spare
spark plugs (the engine of course had eight, two for each cylinder). The horn
would have been chosen by the owner.

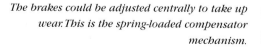

The brakes could be adjusted centrally to take up
wear. This is the spring-loaded compensator
mechanism.

A comparison with the picture of EXP 2 on page 20 makes clear that the front dumb-irons were more gently curved on production cars like this than they had been on the prototypes, which were based heavily on the 1914 TT Humber chassis that Burgess knew so well.

The gearbox was mounted remotely from the engine, and the gearchange lever can be seen on the right, together with its gate, which is labelled with the gear positions. This is an A-type gearbox, with six cover nuts, a cast B on the lid, and the speedometer drive at the front.

Axle number 182 was originally fitted with 13/51 gears, giving a final drive ratio of 3.923:1. This gearing was usually associated with Speed Models on the short chassis, which this car is not.

The dynamo was driven from the back of the camshaft through an arrangement which allowed for engine movement.

The cars incorporated a number of Bentley patents, which were detailed on a brass plate mounted on the engine side of the bulkhead.

A Speed Model chassis – in fact a 1927 example owned by Tim Houlding that is being built up with the specification of a team car. Clearly shown is the overall layout of the 3-litre, with the gearbox mounted remotely from the engine, the dynamo on the driver's side of the bulkhead, and the fuel tank (larger than standard in this case) at the rear.

Front brakes and steering linkage of the Speed Model chassis.

The handbrake, ratchet and spring-loaded adjusting mechanism are clear in this view, as is the gear lever with its neat gate and spring-loaded reverse detente.

Chapter Three

The Later 3-Litres

1925-1929

The 100mph or Supersports derivative of the 3-litre Bentley saved weight by using a special short chassis with a wheelbase of just 9ft. This example, on chassis number 1114 from May 1925, has the special squat radiator that was fitted to about half of the small numbers produced.

Even though Bentley had sold more cars than ever before in the 1924 season – in fact more than in any subsequent year – the company was actually in a parlous financial state. One reason was the cost of developing the new six-cylinder car that WO knew would be essential; another must have been that sales began to slide not long after the 1925 season opened in the autumn of 1924. In *Fifty Years in the Motor Trade*, Bentley sales manager AFC Hillstead remembered 1924 as a year "when the company could not buy a packet of cigarettes without increasing its overdraft".

1924-1925 – the 100mph and Light Touring models

No new Bentley model was announced in autumn 1924 for the 1925 season – the first time

there had been nothing to offer wealthy Bentley fans who eagerly anticipated the latest developments. In fact, there was less on offer than before, as the TT Replica model had now been dropped. The primary 3-litre model was the Long Standard type; the Short Standard was still available but was now rarely ordered and was entering its final season; and the Speed Model provided high performance for those who wanted it.

It was not enough. Exactly when the turning-point came is not clear, but as the 1925 calendar-year got under way WO was obliged to seek clandestine financial aid from Dudley Benjafield, one of his Le Mans team drivers, to keep his company afloat. By this stage, he knew that he needed another attractive new model which would bring in the customers, as well as the new 6½-litre, and he needed it quickly. In practice, Bentley Motors responded to the challenge by developing not one but two new variants of the 3-litre that were brought to market late in the season. These were the 100mph and Light Touring models.

Meanwhile, there were at least improvements for the Speed Model. The engine development work that had been going on at Cricklewood led to a switch in about January 1925 from a single Smith carburettor to the Smith-Bentley 45BVS type, and then shortly afterwards there was a further change, this time to a new twin-carburettor installation. This had twin SU G5 "sloper" carburettors of 1⅜in choke size. The

Speed Model's engine now delivered around 10bhp more than the standard low-compression variant at the same conservative 3500rpm, which may not sound like much to modern ears but represented an improvement of about 11 per cent in peak power.

The 100mph Model, also known as the Supersports, followed in March 1925 and would in effect be the final development of the original 3-litre model – even though 3-litres would remain available until 1929. At Cricklewood, it was already clear that the 3-litre engine had reached the limit of its potential with the high-compression variant used in Speed Model chassis. There were two problems: first, the narrow bore made it impossible to use larger valves to improve the engine's breathing; and second, further tuning of any kind was likely to harm reliability and durability. So, if more power was not readily to be had, Bentley resolved to stay ahead of the game by reducing weight.

This they did by developing a special short chassis with a 108-inch (9ft) wheelbase and fitting it with a special engine which incorporated new drilled hourglass pistons that gave an ultra-high (for the time) compression ratio of 5.6:1 and an estimated 85bhp; the standard 3-litre engine at this stage was delivering around 70bhp. With the Speed Model's tall final drive gearing, the resulting car was capable of a genuine 100mph, although Bentley would issue only a one-year guarantee instead of the five-year guarantee that came with all their other models, perhaps because they anticipated that these cars would be used exceptionally hard. As the 1925 sales brochure put it, "The Company can offer a special short chassis model with a guaranteed speed of 100mph... A limited number of these chassis will be built to special order, and from two to three months will be required for delivery."

Numbers were indeed limited, and this model probably contributed a lot more to the Bentley reputation than to the Bentley coffers. Just eight were built before the end of the 1925 season, the first example being on chassis number 1046. There is some dispute over the total numbers built in the three seasons of the model's production, but the figure of 18 is generally now accepted as accurate.

One way or another, the Supersports version of the 3-litre was limited to an overall weight of 26½cwt (1346kg) to ensure that heavyweight

bodywork could not prevent it from reaching the promised 100mph – which, sales brochures assured buyers, every car could achieve at Brooklands. About half of the Supersports models were fitted with a special squat radiator that tapered inwards at the bottom like that on the new 6½-litre models and bore yet another version of the Bentley badge, this time with a green enamelled background to the winged B. However, the "green label" was no guarantee that a car had the 100mph specification, and would in fact be used on the works team cars from 1928, on many privately-owned 4½-litres seen in major races between 1928 and 1930, and on the Speed Six models as well.

Exciting though it sounded then and still sounds today, the Supersports model was not an unqualified success. Darrell Berthon's 1967 assessment in the *Profile* series of publications was that the car was "tricky to handle at the best of times, being liable to break away at either end almost without warning", and *The Technical Facts of the Vintage Bentley* warns that "this very short chassis was not to everyone's taste and it acquired a reputation of being difficult to handle, particularly in the wet". The book adds that the model was a development of the cut-down chassis that Dr Benjafield had used with some success at Brooklands, and

The performance of the original high-compression engine in the Speed Model was further improved in early 1925 by a change to twin SU G5 "sloper" carburettors. This picture makes clear how they got their nickname. The early type of sump is obvious in this picture from August 1924.

This is why the longer-wheelbase chassis had become necessary. Many customers wanted the reliability, smoothness and performance of the 3-litre, but in an enclosed car. Freestone & Webb built this rather grand saloon in 1925; unpainted bonnet panels were a fashion of the early 1920s.

notes that the 1925 cars (there were others built in the 1926 and 1927 seasons) "were made as an experiment for racing and to special order".

The second of the new models introduced late in the 1925 season was the Light Touring model. This was rather a different concept, and was a car that was manufactured to meet a price – for such things happened and still happen today with products that are way beyond the means of all but the very wealthy. The idea behind this model, which was based on the short chassis, was to offer a fully-equipped 3-litre touring car for under £1000. Its overall weight was limited to 32cwt (1625kg) so that no customer could encumber it with heavyweight bodywork and ruin its performance.

Chassis number 1145 was the first Light Touring model, completed in July 1925 with a special open touring body by Vanden Plas. The same coachbuilder bodied around 20 cars to the same style in 1925-26, and there was a similar number of Light Touring chassis bodied by other coachbuilders. The combination of short-wheelbase chassis, standard engine and relatively lightweight, usually open, bodywork delivered cars with enough performance to maintain Bentley standards while allowing Bentley Motors to offer them at an attractively affordable price.

The Light Touring model of course arrived too late to do much for Bentley's sales in the 1925 season. Figures published by the Bentley Drivers' Club show that just eight were delivered before the start of the 1926 season, which saw the majority of sales. For the 1925 season, overall Bentley sales were down by a total of 10

cars as compared to the 1924 season. Things were not looking good for the company, and all hopes were pinned on the success of the new 6½-litre six-cylinder model that would be announced in the autumn but which, realistically, would not begin to reach customers until early the following year.

An important running change was also made during the 1925 season, increasing the cooling capacity of the radiator and possibly intended mainly to counter greater cooling demands associated with the Supersports cars. There is some dispute about whether the change was made in two stages, but essentially it involved the addition of a header tank to the radiator and an increase in the radiator's overall height of an inch. The header tank was added at or around chassis number 1003, mid-way through the season and about three months before the Supersports car became available with chassis number 1046. The taller radiator was not added until later according to expert Michael Hay, who believes the change was made at chassis number 1092, a car built in the 1925 season which remained unsold and was re-numbered (as NR507) with a 1926-season identity. One way or another, the increase in radiator height was important for other reasons, because it gave a straight bonnet line between scuttle and radiator instead of the tapering line seen on the first cars. Darrell Berthon rightly comments that the cars looked all the better for this change.

A look back over the 1925 season that ended in the summer of that year would not have revealed the true extent of Bentley Motors' problems. Sales had held up quite well, the total of 392 deliveries being only 10 down on the previous year's record. More than half were long-chassis cars, with a total of 240. There had been 130 Speed Model chassis, the same figure as in the previous season, plus eight Light Tourers, eight Supersports models, and six short-chassis standard 3-litres.

The summer of 1925 was also a watershed in the story of the 3-litre Bentley. Up to that point, it had been the only model available from the Bentley stable, albeit dressed up to resemble a complete range by means of such models as the TT Replica, the Speed and the Supersports. At the Olympia Show that autumn, Bentley Motors announced its new 6½-litre six-cylinder model, and although production examples did not get into the hands of buyers before March 1926, the new model rapidly began to have an impact on the old.

Most importantly, the 6½-litre Bentley was vastly better suited to heavy and formal bodies than the 3-litre had been. As a result, the 3-litre was largely deserted by customers who had bought the chassis for such bodywork in earlier years. This left it with a fairly clear role as a rugged sports-type chassis, but as time went on it became clear that the 3-litre was no longer as far ahead of other marques as it had been. From mid-1927, it was joined by a more powerful four-cylinder Bentley, the 4½-litre. The 3-litre lasted in production for another two years, valuable as an entry-level model that kept ownership of a Bentley open to a wider clientele than might otherwise have been the case, but sales gradually dwindled to a trickle and production was finally stopped in mid-1929.

Other events at this time were crucial to the future of not only the 3-litre but also Bentley Motors as a whole. Cash-flow throughout 1925 was a subject of major concern, and by the end of the year it was abundantly clear that the company needed to be bailed out – and quickly. It was the resourceful AFC Hillstead, the Sales manager who knew Bentley's customers personally, who came up with the idea of approaching Woolf Barnato. Fabulously wealthy and already acquiring the playboy reputation that would always stay with him, Barnato was not only a Bentley owner but a regular competitor at Brooklands and a talented racing driver.

On the pretext of demonstrating the new 6½-litre Bentley to him, Hillstead was despatched to Barnato's mansion in Surrey to open negotiations. The upshot of this approach was that in May 1926 Barnato made an offer for Bentley Motors. The offer was accepted and, as WO put it in his autobiography, "the broom was forcefully wielded". Hillstead and WO's brother HM Bentley were among those who resigned. Barnato had saved the company from forced liquidation, but his patience would not last forever. While it did last, he proved himself a first-rate driver in the Bentley "works" team.

1925-1926 – some rationalisation

By the middle of 1925, 3-litre production was outstripping sales. This was not necessarily a bad thing: there is no harm in having a small amount of stock to avoid delays when customers want cars in a hurry. But Bentley

Motors had far too many chassis in stock by the end of the 1925 season, and made sure that these did not lose their appeal by renumbering several of them as 1926 chassis. The Bentley Drivers' Club has identified no fewer than 19 of these, a number which paints a rather graphic picture of how badly 3-litre sales had begun to slide. Nor did they pick up again in 1926, which saw sales of 293 cars (plus 58 of the new 6½-litres). This total was a massive 99 chassis down on the 1925 figure, or something like 34 percent.

There were no more Short Standard chassis for 1926, and the original 9ft 9½in chassis was now available only for the Light Touring and Speed Model 3-litres. The Speed Model now took on the high-compression Supersports engine and a radiator stone guard, the latter inspired by the two Bentley entries for the 1925 Le Mans race, and proved far and away the most popular Bentley that year. The mainstream model, although less popular than the Speed Model, was the Long Standard chassis; and the set of four models was made up by the continued availability of the 100mph or Supersports chassis with its unique short 9ft wheelbase.

This year saw the 3-litre engines take on the one-piece or "big" sump although, as noted above, the date of the theoretical changeover point was much earlier than the date of the last car built with the older style of sump. Tyres changed, too, from the original 820x120 beaded-rim type made by Palmer, Pirelli or Rapson to the latest type suitable for well-based rims. These had a 5.25x21 size and were made by

The 3-litre was certainly not a small car, but this Vanden Plas tourer on the 9ft 9½in chassis is positively dwarfed by the 6½-litre alongside, which is on a 12ft wheelbase. The 3-litre was on chassis RN3046 and was new in February 1928, while the Harrison-bodied saloon is just over a year older. Both cars had the same owner.

Pictured in July 1924, this is the long standard chassis that became standard fare for the 1925 season. The strut gear that reinforced the side members of the frame is clearly visible.

Dunlop. However, cars delivered overseas, where road conditions were assumed to be worse than in the UK, seem to have retained their oversize 880x120 beaded-edge types.

Brakes changed, too. The early sliding Perrot shafts had tended to wear and seize up after high mileages, so Cricklewood modified the installation. The shafts themselves were now fixed in place and the sliding effect was transferred to the frame bracket. That seemed to do the trick.

Other changes on the 1926-season cars were brought about by the arrival of the new 6½-litre chassis. The strut gear on the Long Standard chassis was given strengthening plates and all models took on the stronger four-star differential designed for the more powerful car. Even the chassis numbering system changed at the start of 1926 in anticipation of the 6½-litre's arrival that March and, instead of a simple sequential system, the traditional batches of 25 had two prefix letters followed by a three-digit or four-digit serial number.

1926-1927 – second-best

Once the 6½-litre chassis had become available, the focus of Bentley's whole business shifted

noticeably. The new six-cylinder car sold 127 copies in its first full season on sale, while sales of the various 3-litre chassis in that 1927 season dropped again to 141, just under half of the 1926 figure. The four-cylinder chassis was clearly overdue for replacement, and indeed the plan was for the new 4½-litre model to begin replacing it in the 1928 season. In the meantime, the Long Standard chassis and the Speed Model continued to hold the fort. The 1927 season also saw one final Light Touring and two final 100mph chassis delivered, but orders for these cars had now dried up.

There were, as always, evolutionary changes to the 3-litre. The chassis frames were stiffened through the use of thicker steel (now 0.156 inches instead of the original 0.144 inches), and the gearbox in the short-chassis cars was now the stronger and quieter C-type, as used in the new 6½-litre chassis but with internal ratios that were unique to the four-cylinder cars. Some of the Long Standard chassis also had this new gearbox.

There were also engine changes, to commonise the 3-litre with the newer 6½-litre type and with the forthcoming 4½-litre wherever possible. The most obvious of these was a single-piece casting for the sump and crankcase, which replaced the separate oil tank under the crankcase of earlier engines. Altogether less visible was a change from steel to duralumin for the valve rocker arms, accompanied by separate rocker boxes instead of a single cover for the two sets of rockers. In the beginning, the new duralumin rocker arms gave some trouble, but they were quickly modified on production. The original BM1800 camshaft was again standardised in 1926, after some three years of the

For comparison, this is the 9ft 9½in chassis of the Speed model. The difference in the length of the side members is most noticeable in the centre, immediately behind the handbrake.

BM2391 type. In addition, the magnetos were changed from CG4 to GR4 types at chassis number AX1657 in the first quarter of 1927, to commonise components with the 4½-litre engine that was then on test at Cricklewood.

1927-1929 – The final years

The 1928 season saw Bentley sales rejuvenated by the arrival of the new 4½-litre chassis, although this rejuvenation was really more like a respite: total sales for the 1928 season were 408 chassis, only slightly more than in the 1925 season when figures of that order had failed to put the company in a healthy trading position.

Not surprisingly, the lion's share of 1928-season sales went to the new 4½-litre model. Bentley Motors more or less stopped promoting the 3-litre, and did not bother to display an example at the Olympia Show in October 1927. So sales of the 3-litre dropped yet again, to 46 cars – less than a third of the 1927-season total. The Long Standard chassis accounted for 21 of those, and the Speed Model for the remaining quantity. For the 1929 season, just eight 3-litre chassis found buyers as the model's life came to its natural end. Four were Long Standard types, and four were Speed Models.

Evolutionary changes in these last two seasons of the 3-litre's production life followed developments on the 4½-litre cars and once again bore witness to attempts at standardisation and minimising manufacturing costs. The chassis frames were again made thicker, after cracks had appeared in the chassis of the team cars during the 1928 Le Mans, and now took on the same 0.188-inch dimension as the 4½-litre types. The modified front axle with its heavier beds was also fitted. As for the engine, it took on the separate rocker boxes designed for the 4½-litre, and also the fixed top vertical bevels of the 4½-litre type. The dynamo, too, was changed from the original 10-amp Smith's 2D type to the 12-amp 2DA specified for the 4½-litre engine.

The final car with the full "100mph" specification was LT1587, delivered in December 1926, but one last car with the Supersports engine was delivered in May 1927 on a 9ft 9½in chassis as AX 1652. In combining the Supersports engine with that wheelbase, the car's specification was unique. The customer presumably needed the extra chassis length to accommodate four people, since he had the car bodied as a lightweight Weymann saloon by HJ Mulliner. The

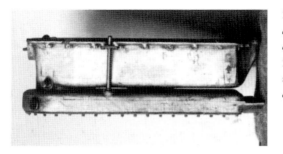

These pictures show the difference between the earlier and later sumps. The "big sump" (below) was fitted on the engines of 1926 and later models.

very last 3-litre built by the old company had chassis number DN1741 and was completed in August 1929 as a four-seat tourer by Wylder, a small coachbuilder with premises at Kew in Surrey.

Yet even that was not the end of the 3-litre Bentley. As Chapter 10 explains, four "new" chassis were supplied to customers through Bentley Motors (1931) Ltd. However, new they were not. The four chassis were actually old frames that had been bought in and reconditioned with new parts as required. What is perhaps most interesting about this episode is that there was still sufficient interest in the 3-litre, a decade and a half after its introduction, for wealthy buyers to lay out their money and purchase one. All four of those "new" chassis were actually sold as second-hand, to avoid misleading customers, but all had brand-new specially-built bodies by Vanden Plas in the contemporary idiom, with a two-door four-seater drophead coupé design.

Driving the Bentley 3-litre

Right from the start, it was the driving qualities of the 3-litre Bentley that made it stand out from the crowd of other manufacturers' products. Even though evaluations in the motoring magazines of the 1920s habitually pulled punches, it is evident from those devoted to the Bentley that the car really was an impressive piece of machinery. To an extent, the search for superlatives tended to obscure the reasons why the 3-litre was so good,

The Light Tourer was introduced at Olympia in 1925 and, though bodied by the respected coachbuilder Vanden Plas, was no thing of beauty. Note the spare wheel outside the body above, which meant there could be no driver's door.

but there is enough evidence in magazines of the time to help us understand how the Bentley gained its reputation.

A consistent theme in contemporary road-tests is the engine's great tractability. It had enough bottom-end torque to pick up smoothly from speeds as low as 6 or 7mph in top gear (although nobody ever talked about torque in those days), and that was something of a revelation. While some of the bigger six-cylinder cars of the time could also do this, most four-cylinders of the 1920s would not have been able to run at that speed at all when in top gear. So several road-tests admiringly compared the 3-litre to a big six-cylinder.

The value of running at such low speeds in top gear was not as a party-trick. The fact was that gear-changing in the 1920s was something of a black art: gear-shifts could be stiff, heavy and awkward, and of course there was no synchromesh to ease the graunching of a mis-timed shift. On this count, too, the Bentley scored highly, and the gearbox was generally considered easy to use. Perhaps that had not always been the case, though, and there is some delightful and very British 1920s circumlocution in *The Motor*'s test of a TT Replica model in its issue of 6 March 1923: "The early model Bentleys were capable of being criticised [in that] a certain amount of care was required to enable changes that were both clean and quick to be effected consistently."

This docility (the word cropped up in several

tests of the time), combined with the car's ability to rush up to high speeds very quickly, gave the 3-litre two sides to its character. *The Autocar* expressed this rather well in its test dated 15 April 1922, when it was let loose on EXP3, the pre-production car with All-weather body that WO had taken for his own use: "The car could be transformed into just what its driver chose to make it; at will a very powerful, ordinary touring car, or very nearly a racing car."

Similar thoughts were expressed in the *Brooklands Gazette* of July 1924, which found the Speed Model just as docile as the standard car and summed it up as "a high quality sporting vehicle which is quite practicable for ordinary touring and exceptionally attractive amongst sporting designs for town and general use".

The two sides to the car's character show clearly why it appealed both to the sporting motorist whom WO had originally had in mind as his target customer, and to the motorist who wanted a car which drove easily enough to be a town carriage. That two-sided appeal influenced the development of the marque from the beginning, and explains why it was eventually forced to make two different cars with similar characteristics: the overtly sporting four-cylinders exemplified by the 3-litre and 4½-litre, and the more deliberately impressive (but no less performance-oriented) six-cylinder 6½-litre and 8-litre chassis.

Contemporary road-tests also showered praise on the steering and the brakes, and even more so on the latter once four-wheel brakes had arrived. However, attitudes and expectations change, and modern drivers are apt to find these controls heavy. Darrell Berthon's view in his 1967 *Profile of the 3-litre* was that "the brakes, considering the weight of the car, were extraordinarily effective; but considerable pedal pressure was required".

As for the steering, expectations had clearly changed even as early as 1933, when *The Autocar* tested an early car (chassis number 239) then for sale second-hand. The magazine recorded that the steering was "high-geared... and heavy on sharp turns, but accurate". Darrell Berthon's view in 1967 was "Although at slow speeds the steering was somewhat heavy, it became easy and light as the speed increased and at all times remained positive. The steering was extremely sensitive to correctly balanced front wheels; each wheel being supplied with four 'studs' on to which lead and fibre rings were threaded and secured with a nut. The tendency of the car was to understeer with the rear end breaking away first but, even on ice, it always gave plenty of warning before things got out of hand".

More recently still, Malcolm McKay drove a Supersports model for *Classic Cars* magazine in its December 1997 issue, and noted, "the steering... is incredibly direct. Forget turning the wheel when the car is stationary – it's simply impossible to turn unless you're on a polished floor. Only a fractional speed is necessary for it to lighten enough to turn, so manoeuvring is not as difficult as it might sound. It's when you have to hold it on lock that the steering becomes seriously heavy – the self-centring pull is incredible".

McKay also made another important note of interest to modern-day drivers planning to drive a 3-litre. He reminded them that the accelerator pedal is in the centre, not on the right as is modern practice!

Looking back

The 3-litre Bentley was at its peak between 1922 and 1926. Sales began to slide as soon as a more powerful alternative in the shape of the six-cylinder 6½-litre model appeared, and they virtually collapsed when the 4½-litre was introduced as a replacement for the original

four-cylinder model. More than anything else, this spells out what most customers saw in a Bentley: it was performance. Once the 3-litre no longer offered the ultimate in fast motoring, the customers moved on to a chassis which did.

Even though the 3-litre's final years can therefore be seen as three years of declining sales, the fact remains that it was the 3-litre more than any other model which defined perceptions of the Bentley marque in the 1920s. It sold more than twice as many as the 4½-litre and around three times as many as the 6½-litre. The small-production 8-litre and 4-litre models were also-rans in this comparison.

An ultra-short wheelbase of 9ft exactly was used for the 100mph or Supersports models. This one is chassis number 1126, for which the Australian coachbuilder Flood came up with a striking two-seater body in 1925. The spare wheel is mounted at an angle in the bodywork behind the seats.

3-LITRE BENTLEY PRODUCTION

Note: These figures are taken from Bentley Motors records. In addition to the production models listed here, there were
4 experimental models (one in 1919, two in 1920 and one in 1922)
13 chassis destroyed by fire in 1924 (at least two were rebuilt and are included in these figures)
4 reconditioned chassis sold in 1936; these are included in the figures below under their first incarnation.

	S Std	L Std	TT	Lt Tr	Speed	100mph	N/K	Total
1921	22							22
1922	130	6	9				2	147
1923	42	130	62		16		7	257
1924		285	1		170		6	462
1925		171			103	11	2	304
1926		104		17	132	6	1	265
1927		46		22	70	1		117
1928		18			16			34
1929		4			2			6
1930		1						1
Total	194	765	72	39	513	18	18	1615

CHASSIS NUMBERS OF THE 3 LITRE CARS

The Experimental cars

There were four experimental cars, numbered EXP1 to EXP4. The first two were built in 1919; EXP3 dated from 1920; and EXP4 from 1922.

The production cars

Chassis were probably allocated to customer orders in strict chronological order. However, the varying times taken by coachbuilders to complete their work ensured that the order of delivery to customers was nothing like the order in which the cars left Cricklewood. So, for example, although the final 1922 chassis was number 149, numbers 39, 127 and 136 were not delivered until 1923, and chassis 1175, sequentially a 1925 chassis, was not delivered until 1927. Some chassis were also re-numbered; eg number 1195, built in 1926, became NR526 in 1927.

Chassis build was initially sanctioned in batches of six, and later in batches of 25, as is clearly apparent from the 1926 and later sequences.

The build sanctions are listed below in the chronological order of manufacture as provided by the Bentley Drivers' Club. The construction of bodywork typically took between two and three months, although some bodies took much longer, and there would have been other delays when Cricklewood sent a completed car back to the bodybuilder for modifications before it would issue the Five-Year Guarantee. Delivery dates shown below come from Bentley Motors records. It would be reasonable to suppose that the actual build date of most chassis was two or three months earlier than their delivery dates.

Bentley Motors were quite strict about recording the points where a new season's specification was applied, and the chassis numbers relating to those seasonal change-points have been listed by Michael Hay. They are listed here in the third column of the table.

For a more precise dating of any individual chassis, it is advisable to contact the Bentley Drivers' Club.

CHASSIS NUMBERS	DELIVERY DATES	REMARKS
1-1240	Aug 1921 – July 1926	First 1922 season car: chassis no 1
		First 1923 season car: chassis no 110
		First 1924 season car: chassis no 352
		First 1925 season car: chassis no 713
		First 1926 season car: chassis no 1083
AP301-AP325	Dec 1925 – Jun 1926	
NR501-NR526	Sep 1925 – Apr 1928	
NR574	(see note below)	
HP376-HP400	Dec 1925 – May 1926	
AH1476-AH1500	Jan – June 1926	
PH1451-PH1475	Feb – Sep 1926	
SR1401-SR1425	Apr 1926 – May 1927	
RT1526-RT1550	Mar – Dec 1926	
DE1201-DE1225	June – Dec 1926	First 1927 season car: chassis no DE1209
LM1326-LM1350	June 1926 – July 1927	
RE1376-RE1400	July 1926 – May 1927	
LT1576-LT1600	Oct 1926 – Dec 1927	
TN1551-TN1575	Nov 1926 – Oct 1927	First 1928 season car: chassis no TN1567
BL1601-BL1625	Feb 1927 – Apr 1929	
AX1651-AX1675	Apr – Oct 1927	
ML1501-ML1525	June 1927 – Aug 1928	
HT1626-HT1650	Sep 1927 – Apr 1929	
DN1726-DN1741	June 1928 – Aug 1929	First 1929 season car: chassis no DN 1728
RC31-RC34	June – Oct 1936	Built from parts: see Chapter 10

Note: NR574 was the Service Department breakdown van, and was probably converted from chassis 574, one of those damaged in the Gurney Nutting fire during 1924.

SPECIFICATION FOR BENTLEY 3 LITRE MODELS

Years of manufacture
1921-1929 (plus three experimental models, 1919-1920)

Build quantity
1615 (plus experimental cars)

Engine
2996cc (80mm x 149mm) OHC four-cylinder with four valves per cylinder
Smith 45VS five-jet carburettor; later Smith-Bentley 45BVS type; optional Claudel-Hobson
Two SU G5 carburettors on Speed Models
Compression ratio 4.3:1 (standard); 5.3:1 (1925 Speed Model); 5.6:1 (100mph and 1926 Speed Model); 6.1:1 (100mph, optional); 6.5:1 (Le Mans)
69-72bhp at 3500rpm (standard engine); 80-82bhp at 3500rpm (TT Replica and 1925 Speed Model); 85bhp at 3500rpm (100mph and 1926 Speed Model); 86-88bhp at 3500rpm (Le Mans)

Transmission
A-type gearbox (standard wheelbase chassis):
2.64:1, 1.63:1, 1.33:1, 1.00:1, reverse 2.64:1
B-type gearbox (long-wheelbase chassis):
3.826:1, 2.073:1, 1.453:1, 1.00:1, reverse 3.826:1.
BS-type gearbox (special fitment with tall third gear):
3.364:1, 1.823:1, 1.278:1, 1.00:1, reverse 3.364:1.
C-type gearbox (1927 and later chassis, also all Speed Weymann saloons):
3.364:1, 1.823:1, 1.357:1, 1.00:1, reverse 3.364:1.

Final drive ratio:		
	Standard	4.23:1
	Speed Model	3.785:1
	(with heavy body)	3.923:1
	Le Mans cars	3.533:1
	TT Special	3.43:1
	Montlhéry records	2.87:1

Suspension
Semi-elliptic leaf springs on front and rear axles; Bentley & Draper friction dampers, except on TT Replica and Speed Models, which had Hartford friction dampers

Steering
Worm and wheel steering

Brakes
Drum-type brakes on rear wheels only on 1922-1923 models; four-wheel drum brakes with twin leading shoes from 1924 season. All brakes with rod operation; handbrake acting on a separate set of rear shoes. Leading-and-trailing shoe front brakes from approximately August 1928.

Chassis dimensions

Wheelbase:	9ft 9½in (standard 1921-23, and on Speed and Light Touring)
	10ft 10in (optional from 1922, standard from 1923)
	9ft (Supersports model)
Overall length:	14ft 4½in (long wheelbase)
Overall width:	5ft 8½in
Track:	56in front and rear
Weight:	23cwt (9ft 9½-inch wheelbase, with four-wheel brakes)
	24cwt approximately (10ft 10in wheelbase)
	22cwt approximately (9ft wheelbase)

Performance

Max. speed:	82mph (*The Motor*, 3 March 1925)
0-55 mph:	15 secs (*The Motor*, 3 March 1925)
0-70mph:	28.4 secs (*The Motor*, 3 March 1925)

Note: Bentley Motors guaranteed 75mph for the long chassis, 80mph for the short chassis, and 90mph for the Speed Model.

Car number RE1400 was delivered in November 1926 and shows the Vanden Plas tourer body at its best on a short-chassis Speed Model. Vanden Plas records suggest that the fabric Weymann-type body panelling may have been black originally, but there is no doubt that this car, owned by James Medcalf, is a magnificent example.

Handbrake and gear lever were always outboard of the driver, and the handbrake was usually outside the body as well on open models.

The eared spinners that lock the wheels to the axles are stamped to show where they belong and which way they should be turned.

The Red Label again features on the radiator of this Speed Model. The magnificent headlamps are by Marchal and are prized items in their own right today.

Nearly as clean as it would have been when brand new, this is the exhaust side of the Speed Model's engine. Note the magneto cut-out box on the bulkhead next to the horn.

The fuel filter was always fitted on the offside of the bulkhead. Note also how the protective webbing is fitted to the bonnet support flange on the bulkhead

The engine number (LT 1580) was stamped into the starter motor housing, and on this car it is the original engine. The letters SS stand for SuperSports and indicate the most powerful engine of the time.

Looking forward, this is the sump of the Speed model's engine. Also clear here are the mounting of the brake rod on the chassis frame and the spring hanger bracket, shaped to prevent the axle moving rearwards in the event of a spring breakage.

Front wheel brakes were standard by the time this car was built. Like the rears, they have finned drums.

Under the bonnet, the Speed Model engine has the correct pair of G5 "sloper" carburettors. Unusually, the bulkhead has been painted matt black.

Inviting… but the door was only shallow in order not to detract from the strength of the body. The B pressed into the trim is typical of Vanden Plas work on Bentleys in this period, the small builder's plate a wonderful period detail.

The dashboard of this car is imposing, elegant, and functional. Only a pair of modern warning lights below the steering column detract from the original appearance. Note how many of the dials carry the Bentley name.

Chapter Four

Coachwork on the 3-litre Chassis

Bentley Motors did not build bodywork; their function was to build chassis and ensure that the bodywork that customers chose to have built on those chassis did not in any way detract from the qualities that Bentley had engineered into them. Yet it was inevitable that certain coachbuilders should become more closely associated with the Bentley marque than others. One reason was that a given coachbuilder was able to construct bodies which were not only of appropriate style but also of appropriate quality. Another was that Bentley Motors themselves had a special relationship with a particular coachbuilding company.

When Bentley Motors introduced their new 3-litre model at the Olympia Show in November 1919, they had no complete car to show. The only complete car at that stage was prototype EXP1 which was in effect what we would now call a "mule" prototype and was not representative of the cars the company intended to sell. To give an idea of how a complete Bentley might look, the sales catalogue contained a full-colour reproduction of the painting that F Gordon Crosby had produced before the first car had been finished, but otherwise there was no reference at all to bodywork.

Another, undated, early brochure again relied on Gordon Crosby's work, and explained: "The Company will not, at first, supply complete cars, but will be pleased to put customers in touch with first class coachbuilders. When a body is fitted to a chassis by another firm the

Company will require to inspect the car before the guarantee can be issued." However, not long afterwards the November 1921 sales catalogue stated: "The Three-Litre Bentley chassis is suitable for open or closed bodies, and the illustrations following give some idea of the various types for which we are prepared to quote." From that point on, Bentley catalogues always illustrated a range of standard body types.

Standard bodies

Obviously, there had been a change in thinking at Cricklewood, and there were probably two reasons for this. First, not every customer for a Bentley chassis wanted to go through the complicated and time-consuming process of visiting several different coachbuilders and obtaining competitive quotations for a particular body style. What many would have wanted was an off-the-peg solution, a car they could buy from the showroom without having to wait for its body to be constructed first. Having a guide price in the catalogue also meant that they had a better idea of what the final cost of their new car would be, since even Bentley buyers had a budget.

Second, it quickly became apparent to Bentley Motors that there were coachbuilders and coachbuilders. They very soon discovered that while they could trust certain coachbuilders to do a good job, there were some whose work was altogether less satisfactory. As WO

Big saloons like this one were the main reason why Bentley chassis had to be made longer, and eventually needed a more powerful engine as well. Chassis number 238 was delivered in August 1923 with a Vanden Plas saloon body, and was used by Bentley's Hubert Pike.

succinctly put it in *The Illustrated History of the Bentley Car*, "Some coachbuilders we found very bad." Problems of this kind would be picked up when the completed car returned to Cricklewood for the inspection that preceded issue of the famous five-year guarantee, but those problems introduced unwelcome difficulties for Bentley Motors and unwelcome delays for customers. Unsatisfactory cars would be returned to the coachbuilder for rectification work before delivery to the customer, and that no doubt introduced tensions into working relationships as well.

So a range of standard body types appeared quite early on, and was updated from time to time to take account of prevailing fashions. Cars to the main styles might be ordered for stock, so that there were demonstrators available and also complete cars to be seen in and bought from Bentley agents' showrooms. Customers were of course at liberty to order whatever body style they wanted and to have it built by whomever they wanted, but the problem with sub-standard work seems to have persisted right through the 1920s. A warning to that effect regularly appeared in Bentley sales catalogues; in this case, it is quoted from the October 1928 catalogue, a fact which makes clear that it had not been possible to eliminate the problems even by that fairly late stage. "Purchasers of Bentley chassis to which coachwork is to be fitted other than to the Company's order should ensure that the coachbuilders rigidly adhere to the detailed body-builders' instructions issued by the Company with each chassis, as a certain amount of trouble and inconvenience, both to owners and the Company, has been caused in the past by neglect in this direction."

Other sales catalogues explained exactly what had been done in creating a range of standard body styles: "The Company does not construct motor bodies but, from experience gained, has designed suitable standard types, arrangements for the construction of which have been made with several well-known coachbuilders." The names of those "well-known coachbuilders" were never revealed in the catalogues, not least because some of the standard styles were built by more than one of them. There would be small variations between one coachbuilder and another, but the basic design would be the same. Examples of this are the early saloons, which were built to a common design by Harrison, Park Ward and others, and the ubiqui-

Despite the airbrushed registration plate, this is almost certainly EXP3, bodied by Harrison's as an All-weather and used by WO himself. The 1921 sales catalogue proposed this as a standard All-weather body design.

tous open sports four-seater, which is always associated with Vanden Plas but was also built by Harrison and several other companies.

We do not know the origins of all these shared "standard" designs, but we do know something of the origins of the standard sporting four-seater design. It seems to have been WO's older brother HM Bentley who sketched this up some time towards the end of 1922. The design was passed initially to a company with which Bentley Motors already had a working relationship – Harrison's in nearby Camden Town. This company built the first example on chassis number 154 for S De La Rue, the then Chairman of Bentley Motors, and it was delivered to him in December 1922. The car was road-tested by *The Motor* for its issue dated 6 March 1923. A second example of this design was then built on TT Replica chassis number 183, probably by Park Ward, and became a Bentley Motors demonstrator. The design clearly went down very well, and in later years, as the relationship between Bentley Motors and the Vanden Plas coachworks in Kingsbury strengthened, so Vanden Plas more or less took over its production.

Variety

However, it is important not to get the idea that there was ever a "typical" four-cylinder Bentley from Cricklewood. As Nick Walker has made clear in his book, *Coachwork on Vintage Bentleys*, the popular stereotype of the Vanden Plas sports four-seater, preferably finished in dark green to look like a Bentley works team car, has suggested that there was. The truth, though, was very different. Although the Vanden Plas body was popular, attractive, and suited the Bentley chassis well, the fact is that it was always among the cheaper options available. Really wealthy customers – especially during the time when only the 3-litre chassis was available – often chose closed bodies that were equipped to the expected luxury standards of the day, and these were very different in character from that stereotype.

As for paintwork, the many photographs that survive of Bentley cars when they were new fail to give an accurate impression because they are universally in the black-and-white format that was the only one available at the time. In fact, 1920s coachwork was a riot of colour, especially on bespoke bodies for wealthy clients. A look through the lists in Michael Hay's book of cars exhibited at the annual Olympia Motor Show in London confirms this, with yellows, reds, blues, blacks, greys, browns, whites, creams and two-colour finishes (typically with the darker colour for the wings and sometimes other elements of the body) predominating. Greens of any shade actually seem to have been relatively uncommon.

Sometimes, no doubt, the customer's choice of bodywork was a big disappointment to Cricklewood. WO had certainly envisaged his 3-litre as an open sporting car, and his choice of such bodywork for the 1919 prototype EXP1 was no coincidence. Nor was the fact that the F Gordon Crosby painting of a Bentley at speed, drawn up before any complete car existed, showed similar bodywork. However, not every customer who wanted the Bentley chassis wanted the

Also by Vanden Plas was this splendid boat-tailed body on TT Replica chassis 263 dating from June 1923. Sadly the car was wrecked in an accident in 1933, but was rebuilt and rebodied, and lives on today.

undoubted disadvantages and discomforts of an open car. Many wanted closed saloon bodies, which were in any case gradually becoming more popular in the 1920s, and they wanted the Bentley chassis because it would give these closed saloons a performance better than other similarly-bodied cars. Maximum performance was not the issue for such customers; they simply wanted the best performance they could get with a body that would seat four or five in comfort. And that, as Chapter 2 explains, forced Cricklewood to introduce the longer-wheelbase chassis for 1923. Then, of course, the extra weight of the longer chassis and the closed body hit performance and so reduced one aspect of the Bentley's appeal. This in turn led to the development of the six-cylinder cars. Customer demand drove the development of the Bentley in more ways than WO probably found comfortable – but it also delivered a variety that Cricklewood alone would probably never have achieved.

Early days

In the early days, it was only to be expected that Bentley would deal with coachbuilders they knew, and that they would direct customers towards those coachbuilders if the customers asked for advice. Bentley & Bentley had some familiarity with several coachbuilders, mainly in London, from providing bodywork for the DFP chassis they imported from France, and the contacts they had made were naturally carried across to Bentley Motors.

So it was that the names of Easter and Harrison cropped up very early in the Bentley story. JH Easter had premises a few doors down from the DFP Service Station in New Street Mews where the first Bentley car was assembled, and they were also the landlords who owned the Bentley premises. They in turn did trim work for R Harrison & Son, who had built a number of bodies for DFP chassis and had certainly built at least one DFP demonstrator for Bentley & Bentley. Harrison's were not far away in Camden Town, and were thus readily accessible. These were both small firms, but they could be relied upon, and the Bentley people knew that the quality of the finished bodies would not let them down.

Another name from the early days was Ewart & Sons, whose premises were also in Camden Town. Ewart's were not noted as body manufac-

Dating from November 1923, this Gurney Nutting saloon body was built on chassis number 405.

turers, although coachwork historian Nick Walker notes that they had certainly bodied a Sizaire-Naudin in 1921; Bentley mechanic Wally Hassan remembered them in Elizabeth Nagle's book as "the geyser people; they made nuts and bolts too in those days; probably still do". That remark was probably not intended to hint at any shortcomings in their work, but rather to suggest that building car bodies was something of a sideline for them. They also seem to have had the contract to supply and fit Bentley bonnet panels.

Nevertheless, choice of bodywork and builder was the customer's privilege, even if Bentley Motors were prepared to make helpful recommendations and even if some of those recommendations in the early days might now seem a little incestuous. The company was, after all, feeling its way. Once its reputation became established, though, the names of some top-quality and well-established coachbuilders began to appear in the lists of those whose credits included Bentley chassis.

We can see this very easily from the cars on Bentley chassis that were displayed at the annual Motor Show, held at London's Olympia and in associated exhibition halls. In 1920 and 1921, the Bentley Motors stand probably exhibited the same car two years running, the actual car being EXP3 (WO's own car) with bodywork by Harrison's. Alongside it in 1921 was a four-seater Torpedo with bodywork by Curtis Automobile Coachbuilders, another small London firm. At the 1922 show there were Bentley chassis on the coachbuilders' stands as well, and the names of Gurney Nutting and Vanden Plas entered the picture. At the 1923 show, there were bodies on Bentley chassis to be seen on the stands of William Arnold, Chalmer & Hoyer, Gurney Nutting, HJ Mulliner and Park Ward. Charlesworth joined the list at the 1924 show, J Blake & Co of Liverpool in 1925, Barker in 1926 (plus Connaught and Offord, both on 6½-litre chassis), and Freestone & Webb in 1927 (plus Thrupp & Maberly and Martin Walter on 6½-litre chassis). Victor Broom entered the fray in 1928 with a coupé-bodied 4½-litre, and Arthur Mulliner followed in 1929, again with a 4½-litre. By the end of the decade, then, almost all the big names in British coach-building, plus a number of second-rank and aspiring companies, considered it advanta-geous to demonstrate an association with the Bentley marque.

WO remembered his favourite coachbuilders many years later when he wrote *An Illustrated History of the Bentley Car*: "One or two were very good," he conceded. "Mulliners were possibly the most satisfactory, especially for saloons, while Vanden Plas were far and away the best for open coachwork." There were, of course, many other companies that constructed bodywork for Bentley chassis, and even the *crème de la crème*, royal coachbuilders Hooper, put their name to some Bentleys. Yet there were many bodies by small and relatively unknown firms, who gained the commission because they were geographically close to a Bentley buyer's home or who, quite simply, were more afford-able than the bigger names. It remains the case that we simply do not know the identity of every coachbuilder who bodied Bentley chassis, and it is very unlikely now that we ever will. What we also cannot do – because the records simply do not exist in enough detail – is to say

exactly how many bodies of each different type were built on Bentley chassis.

So this chapter does not pretend to be comprehensive, or anything like it. Instead, it aims to provide an overview of the main body types available for the 3-litre Bentley chassis. To that end, it looks at the "standard" styles listed in Bentley's own sales catalogues, at the cars which Bentley Motors displayed on their stand at Olympia, and at the cars which the company used as sales demonstrators. While these are far from representing the whole variety of bodies on the four-cylinder Bentley chassis, they do at least give a clear idea of the sorts of cars that Bentley Motors thought they were offering for sale. Also of interest are the cars that individual coachbuilders displayed on Bentley chassis at major shows. While these are necessarily a less reliable guide to what Crick-lewood believed it represented, it is barely conceivable that a coachbuilder would have wished to damage a potentially lucrative rela-tionship with a high-profile chassis manufacturer such as Bentley by displaying a car that did not meet with a least some degree of approval from that manufacturer.

THE SHORT-WHEELBASE 3-LITRE

The original designs for the short-wheelbase chassis were relatively short-lived, and figured only in the catalogues for November 1921 and November 1922. However, when the long-wheelbase chassis took over as the standard type, some of the earlier designs were carried over for the high-performance models on the 9ft 9½-inch wheelbase – notably the Speed model.

Saloons

There simply was not room for four full-sized doors on the original short-wheelbase 3-litre chassis, and the four-seater saloon illustrated in the November 1921 and November 1922 sales catalogues had a two-door, four-light body with a vee-screen. It was fairly typical of the times, and was almost certainly the car supplied on chassis number 1 to Noel van Raalte; probably, then, it had been constructed by JH Easter. It was, said the 1921 catalogue, "a luxurious and elegant carriage". Whether the design was ever built in quantity is impossible to say on the basis of evidence currently known to survive. In November 1922, a complete 3-litre four-seat saloon was priced from £1450.

A Gwynne All-weather body was listed but not illustrated in the 1923-season sales catalogues. This one was built by Vanden Plas, probably in 1922. Note that the picture caption refers to Vanden Plas (England) 1917 Ltd; the company was re-formed six years later as Vanden Plas (1923) Ltd.

All-weathers

WO's own car, EXP3, was bodied as a two-door All-weather saloon by Harrison as early as 1920, and it may be a retouched photograph of this car that was used to illustrate the type in the 1921 and 1922 sales catalogues. The BM registration plate of WO's car was among the elements that were changed with the aid of an airbrush. The design shown in the catalogues was a typical All-weather body of the time. The All-weather was essentially a four-seat tourer, but it was distinguished from the ordinary Open Tourer by providing much more effective weather protection. It had side windows made of glass rather than Perspex side-screens, together with a close-fitting and full-length collapsible top on a heavy wooden frame. Its key benefit was in uniting the pleasures of open motoring with the superior weather protection of a closed body.

Whether Harrison's built any more All-weather bodies on 3-litre chassis is simply not clear, but we know that Bentley Motors ordered a sample All-weather body from Vanden Plas in February 1922. Completed in April, that car, on chassis no 58, had the distinction of becoming the very first Vanden Plas-bodied Bentley. That coachbuilder constructed around 15 more All-weather bodies on the short-wheelbase 3-litre chassis before the end of 1923, some specifically identified as having V-fronts (ie vee-front windscreens), so presumably some may have had flat screens. However, there appear to have been no more after that.

An addition in the November 1922 catalogue was a Gwynne All-weather body, although this was not illustrated. It was probably again by Vanden Plas, whose records show a "straight Gwynne All-weather" in green and black being completed that month. The name of Gwynne denoted a new and lighter from of collapsible top, which used a light steel frame instead of the traditional wooden type. Originally drawn up by the coachbuilder James Young, the design was sold to Gwynne's, who seem to have licensed it to other coachbuilders before selling it on to the accessory manufacturer Beatonson. The Gwynne All-weather body brought the Bentley buyer a worthwhile saving of £50 over the cost of a traditional All-weather body with its wooden hood frame.

Overall, though, All-weather designs probably did not attract many Bentley customers. As the

The standard four-seater had an asymmetric door arrangement; there was one at the front on the passenger side as well as the one seen here. The opening top section of the windscreen was pretty much standard on cars of this period; it allowed fresh air in to cool the car or to help with demisting.

3-litre was making its mark in the early 1920s, so the All-weather body was going out of fashion, and permanently closed saloons took over as the customer's favourite.

Four-seat Tourers

The body style that is often described as the Open Tourer first appeared in Bentley's November 1921 catalogue with the name of "standard four-seater". The body was almost certainly by Vanden Plas, whose records show that they went on to build very many of the type. The November 1922 catalogue priced it from £1375.

Characteristic of this design – though not visible on the catalogue illustration – was an asymmetric door configuration with a full-size door for the front passenger while the rear passengers had a half-height door on the driver's side. The driver himself had to get in and out through the front passenger door, which probably was a better solution than it sounds because the gear lever and handbrake would have obstructed any door on his side of the car at the front. There was a sloping windscreen, and the folding top stowed on top of the body behind the rear seats, under a neat fabric cover. The twin spare wheels were carried, one on either side, beside the scuttle and rested in

The attractive body on this 1923 3-litre was by Rippon. The low rear section had the effect of making the car seem longer than it was, and contained a dickey seat, though the view from there must been rather dull. The tax disc is displayed in the hub of the spare wheel.

the front wings. Interestingly, it appears that Vanden Plas also used this design on other chassis, such as a Crossley 20/70 which they bodied in October 1924.

Sports four-seaters

The "special sporting four-seater", as the 1921 and 1922 sales catalogues called it, was a very different body from the more staid Standard Four-seater. A complete car in this style cost £1295 in November 1922. Probably once again a Vanden Plas product, at least in the beginning, it had "a special narrow body, in which weight has been considerably reduced". Space had been considerably reduced, too: the handbrake was fitted outside the body, and the driver's access to it was aided by a scalloped cutaway in the top of the body. There were no rear doors: rear-seat passengers had to climb up and over the body side, using a step positioned on the leading edge of each rear wing.

Semi-sporting two-seaters

Both the November 1921 and November 1922 sales catalogues for the 3-litre offered a "semi-sporting two-seater" with a double dickey seat. The design was offered and illustrated with a

photograph some months before Vanden Plas built their first body on a Bentley chassis, and so cannot have originated with that company.

The original design, which cost £1275 in November 1922, had a sloping tail containing the two-seat dickey "which, when not used for passengers, will hold a quantity of luggage". The collapsible top folded down on top of the body behind the front seats, and there was a raked windscreen. The steering column also appears to have been raked quite steeply to add to the sporting feel. There was a single door on the passenger's side, and the spare wheel was carried in the corresponding position on the driver's side.

Other coachbuilders produced attractive two-seaters which seemed to sit well within the dimensions of the original wheelbase. One such car became a long-standing Bentley demonstrator with Sales manager AFC Hillstead: rebodied from its original four-seater form to carry a two-seat body by Ewart & Son Ltd to the same design as the 1922 TT cars, chassis number 5 was still acting as a demonstrator as late as 1926, when it was updated with front-wheel brakes to make it more representative of current production cars.

It was a striking-looking car. The bodywork was minimal, with a short rounded tail under which the spare wheel was stowed horizontally and from which it protruded. The wings were typical of the times – slender, flimsy affairs designed purely as mud-guards but with a long sweep at the front which added to the rakish appearance. Hillstead had its aluminium panels scratched and then varnished, in the contemporary fashion, which gave an almost luminous milky-white effect when the light caught it. The wings – and probably the chassis and wheels as well – were finished in a contrasting red. It can hardly have failed to impress onlookers and potential customers alike.

Coupés

The 1922 sales catalogue added a new model on the standard-wheelbase chassis, in the shape of a coupé. What that term meant in the 1920s was a two-door car with a single row of seats; it could have either a fixed roof or a folding top, and often incorporated a dickey seat. The Bentley "standard" offering was almost certainly by Park Ward, and was priced at £1450. The specification promised a folding top, covered in

black enamelled leather, and a flat windscreen. However, the customer could order a fixed roof and a vee-screen if he so wished. The same style, with dimensions suitably adjusted, seems to have been carried over to the long-wheelbase 3-litre chassis as well.

THE LONG-WHEELBASE 3-LITRE
The 10ft 10in or long-wheelbase chassis was introduced as an option in 1922 and from autumn 1923 became the standard size for the 3-litre model. With an extra 12½ inches between axle centres, all of it available for the bodywork, this inevitably demanded some new body styles. Two spare wheels were part of the standard chassis equipment, and most coachbuilders arranged for one to be carried on each front wing beside the scuttle.

Open tourers
Sales catalogues for the 3-litre show that the same design of open touring body was available from November 1922 right the way through until March 1928, which was the last catalogue to feature the 3-litre even though a few cars were built after that date.

The basic body design was drawn up by Bentley Motors themselves, but most of the major coachbuilders ended up building it for them. "Design copied at Bentley works 3rd April" reads a note relating to the first example from Vanden Plas, built on chassis number 619 in July 1924. As always, the catalogues contained basic prices, and customers could spend more by specifying non-standard features. In November 1922, when the long-wheelbase chassis was first announced, a complete Open Tourer cost £1425, but by November 1923 it had dropped to £1375; a second catalogue dated November 1923 shows the price as £1225, and that price then remained constant through to March 1928.

The Open Tourer was an elegant if unexceptional four-door design with a bulkhead stiffening the body between the front and rear doors, and a folding top that stowed neatly flat on top of the body behind the seats. A tonneau cover could be fitted over the rear seats when these were not in use. There was room for five passengers, with three accommodated on a bench seat at the rear, and the driver's seat was adjustable. Behind the front seat was a shallow locker for stowing the side curtains. The two

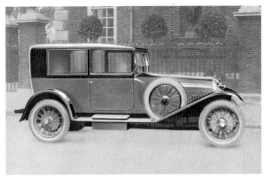

The All-weather body remained a recommended option in 1924 sales catalogues, now for the 10ft 10in chassis. There were still usually only two doors, though, and the extra length gave more legroom in the rear.

spare wheels were carried in the usual location, one on each front wing beside the scuttle. Each running-board had a lockable box, the left-hand one carrying the battery and the right-hand one being a tool box. The windscreen had a fixed lower half and a divided top half, with each top section being hinged to swing outwards.

Worth noting is that there was never a catalogued four-seater sports body for the long-wheelbase chassis. However, this kind of bodywork, invariably built by Vanden Plas, was used on all the four-cylinder Le Mans Bentleys with the 10ft 10in wheelbase chassis, and some examples were constructed to Le Mans specification for private customers as well.

All-weathers
All-weather bodies seem to have been relatively rare on the long-wheelbase chassis, not least because the type went out of fashion in the first half of the 1920s, as permanently closed saloons took over as the customer's favourite.

A two-door All-weather car on the long-wheelbase chassis was listed between November 1922 and July 1925, initially at £1550; the price had dropped to £1355 by November 1923; in October 1924 it was listed at £1355 and £1375 in different catalogues; and on its last catalogue appearance in July 1925 it was £1375.

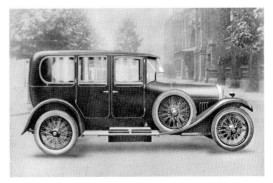

The long-wheelbase chassis gave coachbuilders enough room for four doors and six side windows as well. The vee-shaped windscreen so popular in the early 1920s is still visible on this saloon, which was a standard body in 1924.

Dating from May 1927, this is a Gurney Nutting saloon body on AX1656. The fabric panelling makes a pleasant contrast with the panelled bonnet.

A four-door All-weather made a brief catalogue appearance in October 1925 at the same £1375, but was not listed again.

Vanden Plas records show a number of All-weather bodies on the long-wheelbase 3-litre chassis, beginning in 1923, but the company was presumably not responsible for the original design advertised in November 1922. As for the four-door All-weather, pictures do exist of one built by A Harrison & Sons of Dewsbury (not to be confused with Harrison's in London), but this seems to date from around 1922 and is unlikely to be the "standard" Bentley design listed in the sales catalogue.

In any case, it is debatable how many long-wheelbase 3-litres were given All-weather bodies. The October 1924 catalogue illustrated an example of the two-door design, noting that it had extra-wide doors and sliding front seats to give access to the rear. The screen was a vee-type with adjustable top halves, and the quick-release folding top was made of black enamelled leather. By the standards of the time, however, the design was already looking rather square rigged and dated.

Weymann bodies more commonly had a four-light design because of difficulties achieving a satisfactory shape for the rear quarters when a third side window was present. This was the standard design in 1927 and 1928, and was probably by Gurney Nutting. The dummy hood iron took some of the starkness away from the blind rear quarter panel.

Saloons

There is every reason to suspect that four-door saloons were actually the most common type of body on the four-cylinder Bentley chassis. They certainly figured regularly on the Bentley Motors stand at the Olympia Show, often with the fabric-panelled bodywork that became increasingly popular after 1923. The fabric panels usually indicated that the bodywork was built using Weymann patents.

A four-door saloon was listed in every sales catalogue for the 3-litre between November 1922 and March 1928, with the bizarre and unexplained exception of November 1923. The cost started at £1520, dropped in October 1924 to £1395, and then settled at £1425 in October 1926. The critical difference between the saloons on the long-wheelbase chassis and those on the short-wheelbase chassis was that the longer wheelbase gave room for four doors – plus, of course, more legroom for the rear-seat passengers. The typical four-door saloon also had a six-light configuration rather than the four-light associated with the two-door bodies on the shorter chassis.

Although the catalogue illustrations changed over the years, the basic design of the "standard" four-door saloon clearly did not. Park Ward was building an elegant style from some point in 1923 and the example illustrated in the October 1924 sales catalogue may have been one of theirs. However, Vanden Plas soon got in on the

The long-wheelbase chassis also inspired elegant saloons like this one by Park Ward. It was on chassis 279 and was delivered in August 1923, the month when the 10ft 10in chassis became standard on the 3-litre.

act and certainly bodied the four-door saloon on the 1924 Olympia stand (on chassis number 763) to a very similar design. The Show car was painted in light grey with black roof, upper bodywork and wings – and had silver-plated interior fittings. Later, it would be Harrison who bodied a four-door saloon demonstrator for Bentley Motors. This was constructed in May 1926 on chassis number PH1460.

Either a straight or divided vee windscreen could be had. Drumming was clearly a problem: the October 1924 sales catalogue makes clear that the roof was "specially constructed to reduce vibration and noise" and was "covered with best enamelled black leather". By June 1927, the vee screen was the only option, but the roof could metal or fabric, to choice. Upholstery could be chosen from leather, cloth, or Bedford cord.

Between October 1924 and October 1925, the same body could be fitted with a division (which the 1925 catalogues rather quaintly call a "partition"). This version of the body had a fixed bench instead of two adjustable seats in the front, and was rather more expensive at £1425.

Weymann saloons

The chassis of the 1920s were not very rigid, and as they flexed over bumps and potholes, so their movement was transmitted directly to the bodywork that was rigidly mounted to them. This quite literally led to the bodies falling apart, as well as to unwelcome rattles and squeaks. Charles Weymann, who had been a test pilot for Nieuport in France during the 1914-1918 War, used his knowledge of airframe manufacture to develop a new kind of bodywork that was flexible enough to absorb chassis movements and was also light in weight. Essentially, it had a lightweight wooden framework covered with padding and tightly-stretched fabric instead of the usual steel or alloy panels. Instead of mortise-and-tenon joints, the sections of the frame were joined together with steel plates which could flex slightly. The seats were mounted directly to the chassis instead of to the body, which reduced the need for strength in the body structure.

The first Weymann factory opened in Paris in 1921. In Britain, Weymann began by licensing his system to other coachbuilders, a number of whom took it up enthusiastically. By 1923, demand was such that Weymann opened his

own British factory in London.

All this affected Bentley through three of the coachbuilders who had taken out Weymann patents. These were Freestone & Webb, Gurney Nutting, and of course Vanden Plas. However, the first Weymann saloon offered as standard coachwork on the 3-litre chassis was by Freestone & Webb, and had been drawn up specifically for Bentley. In the October 1924 sales catalogue, it was described as a "Flexible Saloon", with the following explanation: "The Company's Standard Flexible Saloon has four doors, the front seats are of the sliding type and the screen is straight with a divided top half. The interior can be upholstered in leather or cloth to choice." Not all the Flexible Saloons had the same finish: "a good variety both of colours and surface finish is available, from which a choice of panel fabric can be made".

The design of Weymann saloon illustrated in Bentley sales catalogues did change over the years. In the early days, it was Freestone & Webb's rather upright six-light saloon, but in June 1927 the illustration showed a four-light

The Harrison saloon body on the 10ft 10in chassis was pretty much a standard design, though from the middle of the 1920s customers for this type of Bentley would increasingly turn to the 6½-litre chassis.

Six windows and four doors were part of the specification for flexible (Weymann) saloon bodies as well. Again dating from 1924, this is the standard long-wheelbase style. The design may actually have been a "semi-Weymann" type, with metal panelling for the upper half.

The standard early Single Coupé on the long-wheelbase chassis looked like this in 1924; the roof could be fixed or could fold down, and a "three-quarter coupé" version with additional side windows behind the doors was also available.

This is a June 1927 Gurney Nutting coupé body on Speed chassis AX1664. Once again, the outer panelling is fabric.

By February 1928, this design of coupé was being promoted in sales catalogues. Strictly, it is a "three-quarter" coupé, a style distinguishable by the extra side windows behind the doors.

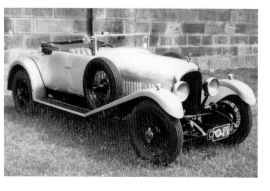

HJ Mulliner built the curvaceous drophead coupé body on long-wheelbase chassis 747 in August 1924.

saloon with blind rear panels adorned with dummy hood irons. The name changed, too: what had started out as a Flexible Saloon had become a Weymann saloon by October 1926 and would remain so. The price started out at £1325, but dropped to £1195 in October 1925. The Weymann saloon was listed at £1325 in October 1926, and then £1350 from June 1927.

Coupés

The long-wheelbase chassis was catalogued with coupé bodywork between November 1922 and March 1928, and in the beginning it looks as if the body on offer was by Park Ward and was a suitably modified version of the style they had drawn up for the short-wheelbase chassis. However, Park Ward were expensive, and by October 1924 a new design by HJ Mulliner was in place. Meanwhile, Bentley Motors had already dropped their price: originally listed at £1520 in November 1922, the coupé on the long-wheelbase chassis had become £1350 by November 1923 and remained at that price until it was last listed in March 1928.

The HJ Mulliner coupé certainly was attractive. It was a perky-looking design, with a tall two-door body typical of the type and a dickey seat behind that was open to the elements. The seating in the enclosed section of the body could be for two or three. The roof was a folding fabric type, with prominent external hood irons.

An early example, and quite possibly the first, was displayed on the HJ Mulliner stand at Olympia in autumn 1924. It was described as having two seats in the main part of the body and a two-seater dickey. The front seat was arranged to slide, presumably to alter the distance from the steering wheel to suit the driver. The car, which has not yet been identified from Bentley chassis records, was painted in "Ciel" (light blue) with black wings and folding top, and had antique brown leather upholstery. Mulliner's referred to this style as the Simplex, and it is interesting that in 1924 it was described as a three-quarter Simplex cabriolet. It is true that the terms cabriolet and drophead coupé were by this time becoming indistinguishable one from the other, but perhaps the term cabriolet was chosen to avoid a deliberate clash with Park Ward who, as noted earlier, were at that stage building a coupé for the 3-litre chassis.

There was no very clear definition of the difference between a Double Saloon and a Limousine, but pictures from the Bentley sales catalogues make clear that the Double Saloon, at least, was a six-light body with four doors. Changes between the 1922 and 1924 were interesting: the earlier car had unpainted bonnet panels in the fashion of the time and the later car shown has a luggage grid at the rear. The back door on the early car was rear-hinged while that on the later car is front-hinged, but this is almost certainly because different coachbuilders were responsible.

One way or another, the HJ Mulliner design prevailed. At Olympia in 1925, the coachbuilder displayed a car largely identical to the 1924 show model and this time called it a Simplex coupé. This second car, on chassis number 1172, must have been strikingly attractive, with its cream coachwork contrasting with bright red wheels and upholstery. A feature of the design highlighted this year was that the cabriolet top folded down flush with the bodywork to leave clean and uncluttered lines; whether it had done the same on the 1924 car is unclear.

By 1926 and its third appearance at Olympia, the Mulliner design was favoured with a place on the Bentley Motors stand – proof, if more were needed, that it had the chassis manufacturer's full approval. This third car has not been identified; this time, it had yet another

Gordon Crosby was called on again to illustrate a closed 3-litre for sales catalogues in the early 1920s. This was probably a Double Saloon – a Limousine would almost certainly have been chauffeur-driven and would therefore have no front seat passenger. This rather delightful picture illustrates the colour schemes of the time better than any black-and-white photograph can. The roof is covered in black fabric, possibly leather, while the wings seem to be painted in a darker shade of maroon than the rest of the body.

description, and was called a three-quarter Simplex coupé with dickey. Surprisingly, perhaps, no record of Bentley Motors fielding a demonstrator of the HJ Mulliner coupé has come to light.

Limousines

There was a degree of uncertainty about where the boundaries between some types of coachwork really lay in the early 1920s, and that was reflected in what appears to be rather loose

Freestone & Webb were responsible for the coupé body on TN1568, delivered in March 1927. The chassis that of a Speed Model, and invisible here is the dickey seat.

Vanden Plas were responsible for this body on an early 3-litre, and called it a Pullman Landaulette. The Pullman name was simply intended to convey the idea of luxury; the car has an internal glass division and was what the Bentley sales catalogues simply called a Landaulette.

usage of descriptions which had once been strictly defined. The Bentley catalogues of the period are no exception, and use a variety of names for limousines of one sort or another.

Strictly speaking, a limousine was a rather grand town carriage, and as such it needed a division between the driving compartment and the passenger compartment in the rear. The precise distinction between a saloon with a division and a limousine is a matter of some debate, but it probably depended to a large extent on the grandeur of the body. A limousine, too, would typically have rearward-facing occasional seats behind the division.

Whether the Limousine listed for £1550 in Bentley's November 1922 sales catalogue qualified for the name on any of these points is something we simply do not know, because it was not illustrated. Nor did it appear in subsequent sales catalogues, and perhaps none were actually built.

However, the type did make a return to the sales catalogues in October 1926, now known as the Enclosed Limousine. It was still available in March 1928, still priced at the same £1435. It was probably a six-light body with an appropriate degree of grandeur – but of course the typical limousine customer was by this stage

inevitably going to be more attracted to the six-cylinder Bentley chassis. The fact that the type remained in the catalogues for a good 18 months suggests that there was some take-up, but it may have been limited.

Meanwhile, what must have been a different style was listed from November 1922 until October 1924 as a Double Saloon. That term was normally used to mean a four-door saloon with a division – and bodies answering to that description were listed as variants of the standard four-door Saloon in October 1924! However, the Double Saloon illustrated in the November 1922 catalogue showed a four-door, six-light design intended "for those who prefer to be separated from the driver". There was also a Double Saloon on the Bentley stand at Olympia in 1923, with its lower half painted cobalt violet, its upper half and wings in black, and its interior upholstered in grey cord. The coachbuilder responsible for this "standard" style has not been identified for certain, but it would be surprising if Vanden Plas had not picked up on the design at some point.

Probably the difference between a Double Saloon and a Limousine, in the eyes of those at Cricklewood, was that the Limousine had rearward-facing occasional seats and the Double Saloon did not. As for the difference between a Double Saloon and a Saloon with division, however, we may never know. Perhaps it depended on what the coachbuilder chose to call his design rather than on any clearly-defined characteristic of the design itself.

Landaulettes and Saloon Landaulettes

A Landaulette was generally understood to be a limousine or a large saloon with a division, and with a folding roof section over the rear seat which allowed the occupants to enjoy the fresh air – or, more importantly, to be seen. A similar style of body without an internal division was known as a Saloon Landaulette.

However, the Bentley catalogues were no stricter in their use of these terms than they were with the various words for Limousine. Sales catalogues for the 3-litre offered a Landaulette body between October 1922 and October 1925. They also offered what they called a Saloon Landaulette in the October 1924 and October 1925 catalogues, adding that it came with a division! For good measure, there was then an Enclosed Landaulette listed from

The open four-seater bodywork recommended for the Speed Model was pretty much the same thing as had been standard wear for the TT replicas. Note, though, the front-wheel brakes on this 1924 car.

October 1926 to March 1928.

Once again, Vanden Plas were certainly in there with what they knew as a Pullman Landaulette that was completed in February 1923 on chassis number 191. Park Ward also built landaulettes on the 3-litre chassis in the first half of the 1920s. Gurney Nutting displayed a four-door, six-light landaulette with division and occasional seats on its own stand at Olympia in 1924. It was painted blue with blue upholstery in what was described as "French fancy cloth". Then in 1925, William Arnold's stand had a 3-litre "Arnaulet" landaulette in primrose and mauve. Yet these body types cannot have been very numerous on the 3-litre chassis, as the fashion for landaulettes had begun to die out in the early years of the decade.

Landaulettes and their sub-variants were always among the most expensive bodies on the 3-litre chassis. Catalogues show the Landaulette priced at £1550 in November 1922 but dropping to £1415 in November 1923 and remaining at that price until October 1925. The Saloon Landaulette was £1450 in both October 1924 and October 1925. Finally, the Enclosed Landaulette was priced at the same £1450 in catalogues issued between October 1926 and March 1928.

TT Replicas and Speed Models

As explained in Chapter 2, the TT Replicas were not exact replicas of the 1922 Tourist Trophy cars. They were simply high-performance versions of the then-standard short-chassis 3-litre, and they could be bodied in whatever way the customer chose. Sales catalogues invariably

showed a car which combined elements of the early standard open four-seater with elements of the Special Sporting four-seater. From the latter it took the lightweight narrow body, outside handbrake and cutaway body beside the driver, and from the standard four-seater it took its door arrangement. Unique were a vertical windscreen – although no doubt this could be varied to suit the customer's wishes – and the mounting of the single spare wheel at the tail. The basic price was £1295, and the coachbuilder was of course Vanden Plas.

Pretty much the same body was catalogued for the Speed Model from October 1924, always realistically described as a four-seater: despite

The short-chassis Speed Model lent itself to two-seater bodywork just as the original 3-litre on the same 9ft 9½-inch wheelbase had done. This was the standard style shown in the 1926 sales catalogues. Surprisingly perhaps, the handbrake was not located outside the body, even though this was still characteristic of a car with sporting intent.

Closed bodies were less common on the Speed chassis because of their extra weight, but Bentley Motors did recommend this lightweight Weymann saloon in 1928's sales catalogues.

James Young made room for four in this tourer on Speed chassis 506, new in February 1924.

The short chassis of the Speed Model lent itself to light sporting bodies like this one by Jarvis, which has two additional seats under the tonneau cover. The original wings would have been more arched than those fitted in this photograph. The chassis is number 1236, delivered in February 1926.

the bench rear seat, there really was no room for more than two passengers in the back. Usually although not invariably called the Sporting Four-seater, it was listed right through until March 1928 and was always priced at £1125. Bentley Motors used one as a demonstrator. This was on chassis number 1019 from March 1925, and was finished in scratched aluminium and black. There were also examples of this design on the Bentley stand at Olympia in 1924, 1925 and 1926. The 1924 car was on chassis number 760 and had Ivory bodywork with blue wings and blue upholstery. The 1925 and 1926 Show cars had chassis numbers 1147 and 1197 respectively, which rather interestingly dates them both to October 1925!

The range of bodies that Cricklewood offered as standard for the Speed chassis was quite limited, although customers of course often indulged their whims and ordered something bespoke. Alongside the Sporting Four-seater, the only catalogued options were a Sporting Two-seater (from November 1923 to March 1928) and a Weymann saloon (from October 1926 to March 1928).

The Sporting two-seater started out at £1100 in November 1923, was £1125 by October 1924 and had gone up to £1195 by October 1926. It stayed at that price until the end. Although it had some similarities with the Semi-sporting two-seater offered on the early short-chassis 3-litre, it was in fact a new design by Vanden Plas with the spare wheel now carried alongside the scuttle and a smaller door on the passenger's side. There were of course more than two seats, because the car came with an extra pair in the

A Vanden Plas boat-tail design on the Supersports chassis: the body was made narrow enough for the gearlever to be outside, as well as the handbrake.

dickey, but with the dickey closed the pleasingly-proportioned lines were exactly as suggested by the model's name.

The Weymann saloon, introduced late, probably met a limited demand for a high-performance closed car among those who could not stretch to a 6½-litre chassis. It was a four-door, four-light design, but was not particularly modern in appearance. In October 1926 it cost £1335, but from June 1927 the price was given as £1350.

Of course, the Speed chassis by its very nature lent itself to individual expressions of taste. Among those of note was the striking boat-tailed three-seater (on chassis number LT1578) built by Barker and displayed on the coachbuilder's own stand at Olympia in 1926.

Light Touring models

As Chapter 3 explains, the purpose of the Light Touring model introduced in March 1925 was to make available a fully-equipped 3-litre tourer for under £1000, and so to attract more sales at a time when they were desperately needed. However, not every example of the Light Touring chassis was bodied in the Open Tourer style specially developed for it by Vanden Plas. On offer in the March 1925 sales catalogue were also a coupé and a Flexible Saloon.

Both of these bodies were more expensive than the Open Tourer at £995, the coupé costing £1175 and the Flexible Saloon £1195. The coupé may have been the Park Ward type carried over from the early short-chassis cars, although its price is suspiciously low and the body was quite probably built elsewhere. As for the Flexible Saloon, this was a pretty uninspired four-light design, with long rear doors that hinged almost directly over the axle. "In this way," read the October 1925 sales catalogue, "a quarter light has been dispensed with, as the passengers in the rear seat can still enjoy a very clear view. Moreover, the position of the door makes it possible to get out of the car with the minimum of exertion." It was probably another Vanden Plas confection.

The Open Tourer was no thing of beauty, either, and the Vanden Plas body has quite fittingly been described as a "bathtub" design. The coachbuilder knew it as the Short Standard Four-Seater, and fitted it to no fewer than 20 of the 40 Light Touring chassis in 1925-1926. It was not at all the same thing as their standard Open

Tourer for the long-wheelbase standard chassis, but was altogether more formal-looking and upright, with heavy-looking wings, a short scuttle and a rather prim valance between the bottom of the body and the running-boards. The single spare wheel was carried where the driver might otherwise have had a door. Two examples did promotional duty for Bentley, one being 1227 (in scratched grey an aluminium) at the 1925 Olympia Show, and the other 1145, the first example, which became a sales demonstrator. For £995, however, it was a Bentley – and in that sense it was something of a bargain.

Supersports bodies

The Supersports or 100mph model was always intended for limited production, and the October 1925 sales catalogue explained that "bodies on this chassis are built to order, and designs and specifications will be supplied on request."

The car illustrated in that catalogue was a racing two-seater built for Woolf Barnato, but was intended to give a flavour of what could be created rather than to show what was already available. It is likely that no two of the 18 Supersports models were identical, and Bentley Motors quoted no prices. Money would have been discussed when a customer placed his order.

There was never any question of squeezing four seats into the comparatively tiny dimensions of the Supersports chassis. However, some more adventurous coachbuilders managed to squeeze three seats into their bodies, with the third seat centrally or offset behind the front two. As far as it is possible to tell, Bentley Motors never promoted a standard body for the Supersports, never displayed an example on a show stand, and never had a Supersports model as a regular demonstrator.

Half of the 40 Light Touring chassis were given this four-seat open tourer body by Vanden Plas. It was surprisingly formal in appearance, and very different from the standard open touring bodies on the long-wheelbase chassis.

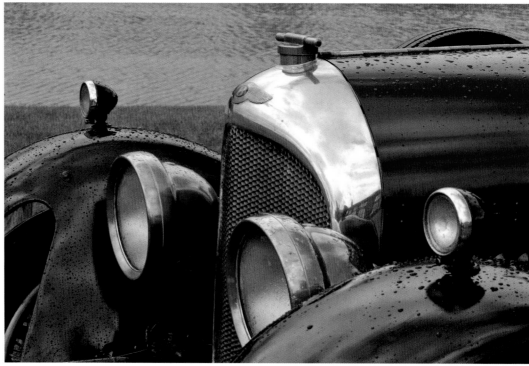

Wonderfully original, and representative of so many bodies on Bentley chassis that have now been lost, is this HJ Mulliner saloon, owned by Tom Pasmore. It is mounted on chassis ML1522 and was delivered in September 1927.

Brass headlamps on this car contrasted with the German silver of the radiator surround, but toned in perfectly with the radiator cap and winged-B badge.

Modern lighting has been added at the rear for safety, and the towball on its bracket was certainly not fitted at Cricklewood in 1927! The luggage rack is seen folded up here, but could be used to carry a trunk when folded down.

Even the door handles, though plain by some standards, were delightful pieces of contemporary design.

The supplying dealer attached this plate to the dashboard.

There are cracks in the leather and the carpets are no longer original, but the interior of this HJ Mulliner saloon is a delightful reminder of times gone by – and of Bentleys no longer with us. Note that the handbrake was inside the body on closed cars like this one.

The 10ft 10in wheelbase was standard on 3-litres by the time this one was built, so there was plenty of room in the back seat. The combination of pleated seat back and plain cushions may have been original, but could also reflect the cost of obtaining pleated cushions when the originals had worn out.

Two spare wheels were carried, one on each front wing. They were supported on neat but sturdy bracketry.

The HJ Mulliner saloon was certainly a grand affair, and no doubt much heavier than WO would have liked, but it was so much more practical than a tourer. It is a tragedy that so few closed 3-litres have survived to the present day in the rush to own an open tourer.

Coachbuilders commonly "signed" their work on the body's tread-plates in the 1920s.

Chapter Five

The 4½-Litres

There was no doubt what WO had in mind when he designed the new 4½-litre model to take over from the earlier 3-litre. It was, as he described it in *An Illustrated History of the Bentley Car*, "essentially a sporting manifestation from the beginning". It also had something akin to a soul of its own, and WO himself described it in the same book as a "hearty, throbbing" car. Bentley Motors' October 1928 sales brochure stressed its relationship to the well-liked and well-proven 3-litre, and

added a few points for buyers to consider: "The car is definitely in that class generally designated as 'sports' models, but it has one very desirable outstanding point common to the Three Litre Bentley, namely, its tractability in traffic, a feature not generally associated with its class. In addition, it is virtually silent for its type."

Yet the 4½-litre Bentley was by no means an entirely new creation. Bentley Motors had neither the time nor the money for that. It was,

Everybody's idea of a vintage Bentley (but see Chapter 7!). This car, on chassis number FB3301, was completed in February 1929 and prepared at Cricklewood for the 1929 Double Twelve race at Brooklands. It was driven by Nigel Holder and Tim Birkin, but failed to finish. The body is a standard Vanden Plas open four-seater, adapted to suit the long 10ft 10in wheelbase. Cycle-type wings had replaced the flowing wings of earlier cars for competition use.

instead, an updated and more powerful derivative of the well-proven 3-litre model. Its chassis incorporated only detail improvements over that of the 3-litre, and was built to the same dimensions: the standard version came with the 10ft 10-inch wheelbase of the Long Standard 3-litre, while a short-chassis version on the 3-litre's 9ft 9½-inch wheelbase was also available to special order. Few customers showed interest in this, though, and as far as we know no more than eight or ten were ever built.

In that carry-over chassis, the key novelty was the new 4½-litre engine, half as big again in swept volume as the 3-litre it was designed to replace and also liable in Britain to rather more annual road tax than the older model. Whereas the 3-litre had enjoyed an RAC rating of 15.9hp, the 4½-litre was rated at 24.8hp. Its annual tax was thus more expensive than the 3-litre's by an amount roughly equivalent to a month's pay for the typical Bentley shop-floor worker.

First run on the test-bench at Cricklewood in February 1927, the new engine was something of a hybrid between the original 3-litre four-cylinder and the newer six-cylinder 6½-litre which had entered production in 1925. So, although it had the same cylinder bore centres as the older 3-litre, its cylinder dimensions of 100mm bore and 140mm stroke were identical to those of the six-cylinder engine. Though always known as a 4½-litre, its cubic capacity was actually 4398cc or, to be as pedantic as Bentley's own sales brochure, 4398.24cc.

The 4½-litre engine shared elements with the four-cylinder 3-litre type it was intended to replace and with the recently-introduced 6½-litre six-cylinder. Visible in this photo by Bentley's regular photographer, Charles K Bowers of Isleworth, are the one-piece sump, twin SU carburettors and the cooling fan fitted to the first engines. The fan was later deleted when the engines were found to be over-cooled. The top cover has been removed to show the valve gear.

The bottom end was almost identical to the 3-litre's, and the engine had the duralumin rockers and one-piece sump that the 3-litre had begun to use in 1926. As on the earlier engine, each cylinder had two inlet and two exhaust valves, as well as two spark plugs. The plugs were fired by twin magnetos, and on the first cars these were the same ML GR4 units as had been used in the 3-litre engines. WO had overcome his initial aversion to SU carburettors enough to approve twin G5 slopers as the stan-

Taken at the same time, this is a 4½-litre chassis. Note the strut gear, and the dynamo protruding through the bulkhead – not normally visible when the car has bodywork.

Yes, it's a Vanden Plas four-seater again – but this delightful example was built for a customer and not for the "works" team. It is on chassis number FS3606 and was delivered in January 1931. The body, covered in black fabric from new, is original. This car also had from new the long bonnet from the 6½-litre, a fairly common option which was thought to make the car look more powerful.

dard issue (as on the Speed versions of the 3-litre) for these first engines.

In case that word "hybrid" gives the wrong impression, it is worth explaining that the cross-fertilisation between four-cylinder and six-cylinder Bentley engines had been the result of sensible production rationalisation. It enabled the two 1928-season Bentley engines to share a number of components so that manufacturing costs were contained. Obviously, running improvements made to the 3-litre engine since its production had begun were also incorporated in the design of the 4½-litre, with the result that the new engine represented the best that Bentley Motors could deliver at that stage in its history, short of designing the completely new engine which it had neither the money nor the resources to tackle.

Specifically, the new four-cylinder engine shared with the six-cylinder its pistons, con-rods, valves, valve stem collars and valve rockers, as well as sundry other items. The design of the 6½-litre engine had also inspired the valve-gear, the magneto and water-pump drive, and the sump, although the actual dimensions of these items differed on the 4½-litre engine. The combination of some older design elements with some newer ones was not allowed to compromise the design, although it did have some effect on it. So, for example, the four-cylinder engine's block was shorter top to

bottom than the six-cylinder by 8mm, with the result that fitting pistons designed for the six-cylinder engine into the four-cylinder raised the smaller engine's compression ratio from the 4.4:1 of the 6½-litre to 4.8:1 in the 4½-litre.

That was no problem, of course, and in fact the Bentley team decided to make a virtue out of it. They decided to offer the 4½-litre engine in two different states of tune, a high-compression (4.8:1) type with 110bhp and a low-compression type (produced by adding a compression plate that increased the height of the block to give 4.6:1) delivering somewhere around 100-105bhp. Later, special versions of the engine were created by machining the crankcase and block and fitting high-compression pistons. For competition use, Cricklewood developed a 4½-litre engine with a 6.0:1 compression ratio and an output of 125bhp at 3500rpm, and for the Le Mans team cars they upped this to 130bhp at the same crankshaft speed by raising the ratio to 6.12:1.

Also notable was that the 4½-litre engine was fitted with a larger-capacity radiator matrix than the 3-litre, as well as a cooling fan, in anticipation of the need for better cooling to counteract greater heat generation. In practice, though, the early engines proved to be overcooled, and there would be further cooling modifications in production.

The rest of the drivetrain incorporated some new features, too. The standard rear axle ratio was 3.533:1, considerably taller than on the 3-litres with their standard 4.23:1 gearing and actually the same as had been used on the Le Mans 3-litres. This was made possible by the fact that the engine put out a lot more torque than the older four-cylinder (although torque was little understood by the public in those days and was never quoted in Bentley sales literature).

The gearbox was a new version of the proven four-speed type. Known as the C-type, its ratios stood mid-way between those of the original A-type gearbox and the wider-spaced set of the B type gearbox associated with the Long Standard 3-litre chassis. Once again, it was the increased torque of the engine that made this modification possible. In fact, the closer ratios of the A-type gearbox could be had to order, although the A-type gearbox itself must have been considered unable to take the strain because for the 4½-litre a very similar set of close ratios would later be made available in yet another new gearbox.

There was a further mixture of old and new in the rest of the chassis. Old were the cone-type clutch with Ferodo lining and the Smith's double-pole electrical system for lighting and starting. New was the 16-gallon fuel tank in place of the 3-litre's 11-gallon unit. No doubt this change was made in anticipation of the bigger engine's greater thirst, although the 4½-litre turned out to be not that much thirstier than the 3-litre.

Perhaps most interesting was that the new and more powerful engine enabled Bentley Motors to raise the weight limit for the 4½-litre cars. The Bentley Drivers' Club's invaluable *The Technical Facts of the Vintage Bentley* notes that the overall weight of open-bodied cars was limited to 32.5cwt (1651kg) but that the maximum permissible with closed bodywork was 37cwt (1880kg). With a chassis weighing 27cwt (1372kg) in standard 10ft 10-inch wheelbase form, that allowed coachbuilders quite a lot of flexibility. It was necessary, too, as fully enclosed bodies became more popular towards the end of the 1920s.

1927-1928 – the first models

The first 4½-litre Bentley was ST3001, which was really an experimental car and which ran as a team car at Le Mans in June 1927. It seems to have had a 3-litre radiator, and it was perhaps as a result of experience during the Le Mans event that a larger-capacity radiator matrix with a

bigger radiator shell to accommodate it (and consequently, different mountings) was fitted to production cars from the fourth chassis. The first nine examples supposedly had a smaller-diameter radiator filler cap than was later standard, although the majority were modified in service to have the later type.

Production chassis began to appear in July and August 1927, and brought no major surprises. Known bodywork did not deviate significantly from the types or even the designs already familiar from the 3-litre chassis, which of course remained available even though now manufactured in only penny numbers. It was

This was the Vanden Plas stand at the 1928 Olympia Show. The cars, advertised as 1929 models, are XR3334 and XR3335, the latter proudly described as an "All British Exhibit".

Vanden Plas delivered this rather attractive two-seater with dickey seat on chassis RN3049 in February 1928.

Harrison had been bodying Bentley chassis since the earliest days, and was responsible for the four-seater body on HF3184 in April 1928. The fabric panelling is evident here; the doors are remarkably narrow and the car carries fashionable wheel discs.

interesting that Bentley Motors liked to maintain the illusion that there was an exclusivity about the new 4½-litre chassis, and an April 1928 sales brochure maintained that it was "being manu-factured in limited numbers". Those numbers certainly may not have been as high as Crickle-wood might have liked, but they could hardly be described as "limited". The 1928 season saw 263 chassis delivered, all but three of them on the 10ft 10-inch wheelbase, which made the new model Bentley's best-seller by far: the same year saw just 99 6½-litres and 46 3-litres leave the Cricklewood works.

The usual procession of running modifications began in autumn 1927 after about 45 chassis had been built, when the over-cooling problem was addressed by fitting a thermostat to control water temperature at chassis SL3071. Then, towards the end of the year, the original rigid-spoke steering wheel was replaced by a Bluemel spring-spoke type at chassis number RN3035. This change did not meet with universal approval; as Darrell Berthon and Anthony Stamer put it in their *Profile of the 4½-litre Bentley*, the new wheel "felt much better from the handling point of view, but at first was disliked due to the danger of the spokes breaking in an accident and the steering column causing serious chest injuries (unlike the rigid spoked wheel which spread the shock over a wider area)".

All the first 4½-litre chassis had the same type of propshaft as the 3-litre, with a plunging joint

whose blocks and slippers tended to wear and also required regular lubrication. Whether the wear was accelerated with the bigger engine is not clear but, one way or another, February 1928 brought the change at chassis number NT3131 to a proprietary Hardy Spicer enclosed splined propshaft, which was of course balanced as well. At the same time, new Bentley and Draper shock absorbers were standardised and the rear axle shafts gained hardened tips.

Later the same month, Cricklewood tackled a problem with difficult starting on the 4½-litre, one which had clearly caused some owners to end up with flat batteries. So with effect from chassis HF3192, the problem was addressed in two ways. The poor starting itself was tackled by fitting a Ki-gass injector – in effect a primer pump that injected neat fuel into the cylinders to aid starting – and the battery drain was tackled by a switch from GR4 to ER4 magnetos.

Just a few chassis later, at HF3196 in March, three more running modifications arrived at the same time. The wearing properties of the brake drums were improved by a change from mild steel to steel with a 44% carbon content, and the engine's floating-type gudgeon pins were changed for gudgeon pins secured by circlips. This modification proved to be a minor disaster, however, because the circlips tended to work loose and score the cylinders, so Cricklewood soon reverted to the earlier design with floating gudgeon pins.

Most important of those changes at HF3196,

Perhaps the archetypal 4½-litre had a Vanden Plas four-seat open sports body. This one, delivered in June 1928 on chassis TX3239, was originally finished in blue. It now sports a modern replica of its original body style.

however, was a new gearbox. This was known as the D-type, and replaced the C-type used from the start of 4½-litre production except on chassis fitted with heavy bodies. Essentially, it was a close-ratio gearbox with a taller third gear and was designed to give a more sporting drive than was available from the more widely-spaced ratios of the C-type gearbox. Its gear ratios were in fact identical to those of the original A-type gearbox used in the 3-litre, but the gearbox as a whole had been completely redesigned so that it could handle the greater torque of the bigger engine.

It also incorporated all the improvements and the lessons learned since that original gearbox had been drawn up some eight years earlier. The main and lay shafts were multi-splined and had reduced overall lengths to minimise distortion under maximum loadings, while the outer casing was ribbed and generally of sturdier construction than earlier gearboxes. On the left-hand side of the casing were an oil filler and the speedometer drive, which latter had nevertheless been redesigned from its C-type configuration. The gate, too, was different, with increased dimensions of 3in x 4¾in as compared to the 2¾in x 2¾in of the C-type gate.

A few chassis later, and still probably in March 1928, the 4½-litre engines were treated to new pistons (the BM3622 type) which raised the compression ratio. The first engine with these pistons was number KM3081 which, unusually for Bentley, was fitted into the chassis with the same number. The standard compression now

went from 4.8:1 to 5.3:1, and the low-compression engine with its 13swg compression plate was now claimed to operate at 5:1 (some sources give the figure as 5.1:1). In theory, these raised compressions would have improved both fuel economy and power, although it is difficult to put actual figures on either measurement.

Plans were afoot by the spring of 1928 to improve the brakes, too, although the changes seem to have been introduced in two stages. The works team cars had been used to try out a system where the operating levers of the front brakes were reversed so that, as torque reaction caused the axle to wind up on its springs, the brakes were pushed on harder. The "production" version of this would be the leading-and-trailing shoe brakes which would

This 4½-litre saloon remains unidentified, but is another example of the fabric-panelled bodywork that was so common in the later 1920s.

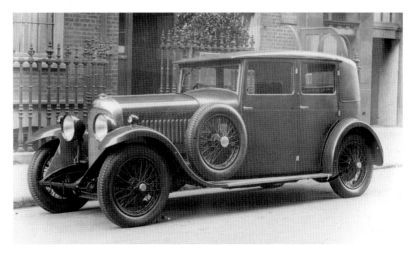

Fabric panelling is again evident on this Vanden Plas saloon body built in December 1928 on UK3288. The light-coloured wheels set off what otherwise might have been a sombre-looking creation.

be fitted to the 1929-season chassis, but these required a reinforced front axle to counteract the increased torque from the new brakes. The new axle was available before the rest of the braking system, and from chassis KM3092, delivered in May 1928, the front axle beam was made of reinforced H-section steel with a thicker section between the spring pad and the swivel-pin eye.

1928-1929 – improvements

The October 1928 sales brochure for the 4½-litre cars still maintained that the chassis was "being manufactured in limited numbers". Perhaps this was simply laziness on the part of the copywriters, who had made minimal changes since the April catalogue; perhaps it was once again a way of making the Bentley sound more exclusive. At that stage in its existence, Bentley Motors was certainly in no position to limit production artificially. Other factors did limit sales to a degree, however, and the 256 examples of the 4½-litre model that found buyers during the 1929 season were slightly fewer than in the car's first season. Just four of them were on the short, 9ft 9½-inch, wheelbase.

For the 1929 season, a key change was to a reinforced chassis frame. This was brought about when two of the team 4½-litre cars suffered chassis fractures during the June 1928 Le Mans event, and for 1929 heavier-gauge metal was specified for the chassis frames. It obviously made sense to simplify manufacture by sharing this new chassis frame with the 3-litre that was in production at the same time, and Chapter 3 explains how the frame of that

model also changed to a 0.188-inch (3/16-inch) gauge. The thicker metal was supplemented by a series of gusset plates and by deeper flanges on the chassis bottom rail.

Cricklewood also tackled a problem that had been looming for some time now, and this was that closed bodies tended to magnify an exhaust boom. WO himself referred to this, and so did some of his team when Elizabeth Nagle interviewed them more than 30 years later, so it must have made a lasting impression. Perhaps the problem was worse with the 4½-litre engine than it had been with the 3-litre, which was why the issue came to a head at this stage. Whatever the reason, chassis destined for closed coachwork – and Bentley sales literature was most insistent that buyers had to specify the type of coachwork they intended to fit to the chassis they were buying – were fitted for the 1929 season with a double exhaust silencer which was designed to cure (or at least reduce) this noise.

Most of the 1929 cars also had a new electrical system, which had entered production in time for the Motor Show at Olympia which opened towards the end of October. Once again made by Smith's, from chassis XR3329 it changed to a fused single-pole system. Further changes arrived just a few chassis later at number XR3332 – although in practice this car was not completed and delivered to its first owner until December that year. These changes included the completion of the braking improvements, as the original twin-leading shoe brakes gave way to what Cricklewood called "self-energising servo" brakes. That rather grandiose description (and others are also used, such as "semi-servo" or "self-wrapping" brakes) simply indicated that the new brakes had leading and trailing shoes. With XR3332 also came the important change from the old-style cone clutch to a more modern plate-type clutch.

The plate clutch and "semi-servo" brakes had both been seen on the 1928 Le Mans team cars, which also had twin vertical SU carburettors in place of the "sloper" G5 SUs on production engines. At XR3332, the production engines also switched to the new vertical carburettors, known as the HVG5 type. The other important engine changes at this stage were intended to improve cooling by reducing the amount of sludge that tended to build up inside the cooling system. At Cricklewood they had discovered that much of this sludge was actually decomposed aluminium which had come from the water-jacket plate or from the water pump body. A switch to Staybright sheet steel for the water-jacket plate reduced this item's tendency to perforate, and at the same time a more corrosion-resistant aluminium alloy was introduced for the manufacture of the water pump body.

Aluminium alloy now seemed to be rather out of favour in general. As 1929 opened, Bentley Motors embarked on a programme which would see many formerly aluminium alloy components change to Electron, an alloy of aluminium with a very high magnesium content. The changeover took several months and began with the bulkhead. It was carried out progressively, and was complete before the start of the 1930 model-year.

The first quarter of 1929 also seems to have seen the old problem of heavy bodywork raising its head again. There had been an interim solution: the D-type gearbox had been created to deliver the best possible performance, but now the C-type gearbox with its more widely-spaced ratios became standard again at chassis number UK3278, which was delivered in March. The close-ratio D-type box of course remained available to order.

The final 1929-season modifications were all carried out over the summer, and all were intended to improve the durability of the 4½-litre engine. There had been some problems with the white metal on the direct-metalled con-rods cracking, and to counter this a change was made at engine number NX3456 (which was fitted to chassis NX3454, delivered in May). This and subsequent engines had separate steel shell big-end bearings, lined with white metal as was customary for the period. The lubrication of the big ends was also improved, drawing on competition experience, and the rocker casings were altered to provide an oil-bath for the rocker rollers.

1929-1930 – decline and (nearly) fall

For the 1930 season, the 4½-litre should have benefitted from the fact that its key rival – Bentley's own 3-litre – had gone out of production in August 1929. However, there were factors at work beyond the control of Bentley Motors. Just three days after the opening of the Olympia Motor Show in October, where Bentley had their usual stand, share prices on the Wall Street stock market in New York collapsed. Those who did not move fast enough lost huge amounts of money, and those who did cash in their remaining shares found that their value had dropped catastrophically. The individuals most affected by these events were mostly the very wealthy, and the very wealthy were Bentley's target customers. As the effects of the crash began to be felt around the world, potential customers reined in their spending. These factors certainly affected sales of the 4½-litre cars in the 1930 season, and they may well have limited the amount that Bentley Motors was willing to spend on modifications to its existing models, too. Cash was certainly tight.

The season opened with minor modifications introduced at chassis number XF 3514, which was delivered in November 1929. The half-shafts were redesigned and strengthened, and the double-silencer arrangement intended for chassis destined for closed coachwork went out in favour of a new Pulswell silencer. This seems to have been fitted to all subsequent chassis, no doubt to simplify production and save a little on costs.

Production simplification and cost-saving were also behind a change which occurred in the first quarter of 1930 and which was a direct result of Bentley's obligation to build 50 production versions of the supercharged cars so that the latter could go racing, as explained in Chapter 6. The supercharged 4½-litre engines needed a more robust crankshaft to withstand the additional stresses imposed by the supercharger, and to suit that new crankshaft they also needed a modified crankcase. It made good sense in production terms to use the same crankcase and crankshaft on the non-supercharged engines and so, no doubt despite misgivings from WO himself, 4½-litre engines built from around February 1930 took on the so-called "heavy" crank plus the Blower's crankcase and cylinder block with its more widely set main bearing studs. The first engine to the new pattern was numbered AD 3651, and this was fitted into a short-wheelbase car with chassis number PB3547 for the Marquis de Casa Maury, who was at that stage joint Managing Director of Bentley Motors. The car was built to full Le Mans specification and was one of the very few examples of this type that Cricklewood ever built.

The "heavy" crank certainly was heavy by comparison with the earlier type, weighing 72lb

At bottom right, this photograph bears the unmistakable stamp of Jack Barclay, the London dealer, so the car must have passed through his hands at some stage. The chassis is MR3377, delivered in April 1929 with this Vanden Plas saloon body.

as against the original's 47lb. However, it was not actually identical to the type used in the supercharged engine, because the spigot for the supercharger drive was redundant and was therefore cut off before the engines were assembled.

Some commentators argue that the "heavy" crank took the edge off the engine's performance. However, it did bring one advantage and that was to make the engine even smoother than before – no bad thing in a large-capacity four-cylinder.

Nothing more changed before the early summer, when there was a further increase in the carbon content of the brake drums (it was now up to 55%) from chassis number FS3602, delivered in June 1930. Shortly after that, engine

number FS3611 (fitted into chassis FS3612) became the first to have a reinforced Electron alloy sump.

WO and his fellow directors must have been dismayed as they surveyed the picture at the end of the 1930 season. Sales of the 4½-litre cars had dropped to less than half of their 1929-season total, and of the 124 non-supercharged chassis built only one was on the shorter 9ft 9½-inch wheelbase. The more expensive 6½-litre was maintaining its sales, more or less, but the overall numbers were not enough to put Bentley Motors in a healthy financial position.

1930-1931 – the final cars
The summer and autumn of 1930 were a critical period for Bentley Motors. While the

This is another Jack Barclay photograph, this time showing NX3454, delivered new in May 1929 with a saloon body by HJ Mulliner.

This 1930 4½-litre on chassis number AD3658 was bodied by Charlesworth when new, supposedly as a saloon. This picture shows it with a drophead coupé body which was clearly beginning to show signs of age: note how the mould lines of the door no longer line up with the rear bodywork. The chassis still survives, but has now been fitted with a Le Mans replica body.

4½-litre chassis remained in production, its falling sales are a clear indication that it may not have had very long to live even if the receivership of Bentley Motors during 1931 had not brought about its sudden death. For the 1931 season, the 6½-litre ceased production, to give way to the new 8-litre six-cylinder, and a new "smaller" Bentley was introduced. This was the 4-litre, with another six-cylinder engine, and it might in due course have taken over from the 4½-litre – even though its character was very different indeed.

Sales of the 4½-litre were depressingly slow during the 1931 season, and just 19 chassis were built, the first eight completing the FT sanction that had been started at the end of the 1930 season, and the other 11 being the start of the XT sanction that was never completed. All of them were on the 10ft 10-inch wheelbase chassis, which may in itself have been a grim reflection of the fact that Bentley customers were in no mood for the frivolities of short-chassis cars with sporting bodywork. They did not have the money to spare, and Bentley Motors suffered for it.

There was just one specification change made to the 4½-litre during the 1931 season, and that occurred at engine number XT3627, fitted to the chassis of the same number and delivered in February 1931. The change was a straightforward reinforcement to the crankcase: right to the end, Bentley Motors was determined to ensure that longevity and reliability remained characteristics of its products.

Vanden Plas again delivered an attractive two-seater with dickey on FS3604, which reached its first owner in July 1930.

The end of Bentley Motors

From the earliest days of their existence, Bentley Motors had suffered from an inadequate cash-flow. Bailed out in 1926 by Woolf Barnato, they had struggled on, but the situation had never improved to any significant degree. Some commentators have argued that the cost of the racing programme was the key factor in the company's eventual demise, but this is not the place to evaluate the pros and cons of that; a fuller account of the end of Bentley Motors is given in the companion volume to this one, which covers the six-cylinder cars.

What was undeniable was that by the start of 1931 the company was in crisis. Woolf Barnato decided that he could no longer prop up Bentley Motors, much as he might have liked to. On 10 July 1931 he appointed a receiver, and the news appeared in *The Times* a day later. The Receiver's recommendation was that the company should be wound up voluntarily because its liabilities were too great to allow it to continue trading.

What happened next was quite complicated but, briefly, things were moving comfortably in the direction of the motor manufacturer Napier buying the Bentley assets. WO himself believed it would happen, and had even done some work on a new car for them. However, when it came to legalising the deal in court, the British Central Equitable Trust Ltd intervened with an offer higher than Napier's. A rather unseemly bidding war followed until the judge announced that he was not an auctioneer and would adjourn until later in the day when he would receive sealed bids.

When the sealed bids were opened, it was the British Central Equitable Trust who had bought Bentley Motors. In due course it became apparent that the Trust actually represented Rolls-Royce. What had once been Bentley Motors became Bentley Motors (1931) Ltd, and a whole new breed of Bentleys, which shared major components with Rolls-Royce models, began to reach the showrooms at the end of 1933.

However, that was not quite the end of the 4½-litre. As Chapter 10 explains, six more 4½-litre chassis were built up from parts in stock during the summer of 1936 and, although they were all bodied in a very different idiom from their forebears, they showed that the old 4½-litre still enjoyed a powerful appeal five years after the last one had left the Erecting Shop at Cricklewood.

Driving the 4½-litre Bentley

The motoring press seems not to have been clamouring to road-test the 4½-litre car when it was first announced, perhaps because it was not an all-new model but rather a re-engined derivative of a car they had already tested. The earliest test appeared in *The Motor* for 8 May 1928, and that magazine's only real rival, *The Autocar*, waited until its issue of 22 February 1929 to try an example. Both magazines were deeply impressed, and both evaluations conveyed a genuineness that was often absent from the polite appraisals of other cars at the time.

"If its specification be put down coldly on paper," wrote *The Autocar*, "it suggests at once a machine which is not of the most modern type." However, "the car cannot be criticised simply in terms of its specification, and that is a point which strikes one most forcibly after a long trial run." *The Motor* was impressed by the Bentley's build quality, noting that "the chassis throughout is most substantially constructed, with beautiful workmanship noticeable in every detail". The focus of this magazine's comments, however, was on the engine and the performance it delivered. "The engine runs smoothly for a 'four' at all except the lowest rates of revolution, and has a high degree of mechanical silence... The charm of this car on a long, fast main-road run is partly due to the low revolution speed of the engine; thus at 60mph the Bentley can be kept cruising for mile upon mile with the throttle only slightly open and an immense reserve of power ready for hills or acceleration."

The Autocar agreed: "The extraordinary feature is that the big four-cylinder will run on top gear as though it were a six, with only the

	4½-LITRE BENTLEY PRODUCTION		
	Note: These figures are taken from Bentley Drivers' Club records. They relate to "season" and not to calendar year.		
	10ft 10in	**9ft 9½in**	**Total**
1928	260	3	263
1929	252	4	256
1930	123	1	124
1931	10		10
Total	645	8	653

curious and not unpleasant torque effect to show that there are but four cylinders in the power unit". Overall, "given an enthusiast as pilot, then the power, speed and, what can only be called the tractability, of the big machine are simply wonderful. It has a feeling of tremendous power that, say what one may, is extremely pleasant". *The Motor* wrote of the car's "lightning get-away" and "rocket-like acceleration", adding that "in traffic the car can be made to leap ahead whenever an opportunity presents itself in a fashion which quite spoils the driver for a return to a slower vehicle".

The Motor pointed out that "the driver must be prepared for frequent gearchanges," but added that the quality of the change did not make this an unpleasant chore, while *The Autocar* felt that "the gearchange could not possibly be better or more delicate." The steering had "a nice, self-centring action" according to *The Motor*, and was "delightful... light, direct and very certain" in *The Autocar's* view. Both magazines praised the brakes. They were "excellent... powerful and yet light" (*The Motor*); "very powerful indeed... added to which they are sensitive and, however violently applied, are not uneven" (*The Autocar*).

The Motor wrote of "road-holding extraordinary", but *The Autocar* warned that "to obtain the car's full maximum the shock absorbers

Owned by David Lawson, XL 3121 is a Vanden Plas-bodied tourer of the familiar pattern. Visible below the frame is the strut gear associated with the 10ft 10in chassis. Note also the uninterrupted row of louvres on the 4½-litre bonnet; on 3-litres, there were two groups with a space between them.

XL 3121 gets well used, as the stickers on the running-board tool box suggest. The auxiliary driving lights were of course not part of the standard specification.

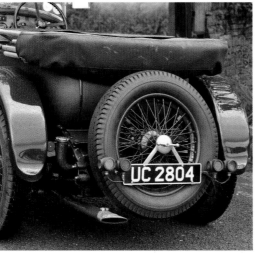

The deeper radiator matrix of the 4½-litre is clearly visible in this head-on picture of XL 3121, which was delivered in April 1928.

The 4½-litre chassis was fitted with a 16-gallon fuel tank in place of the smaller tank used on the 3-litre. The fishtail exhaust visible here was not standard, but a much-liked period accessory.

have to be kept tight - tighter, that is, than they should be for comfortable town work or for ordinary towing. With the shock absorbers tight the car holds the road as though glued to it".

"Ease of control" stood out for *The Motor*, along with "a well-nigh perfect driving position", while *The Autocar* stressed that the car had "two totally different characters", which allowed it to be both docile town carriage and fast sporting machine. But, *The Autocar* summarised, "it is one of the most pleasant existing cars to drive, and a driver in tune with it knows that he has full control... it is as a whole, and very much as a whole, that the 4½-litre Bentley appeals. In that appeal there is something more of the living animal than in most cars."

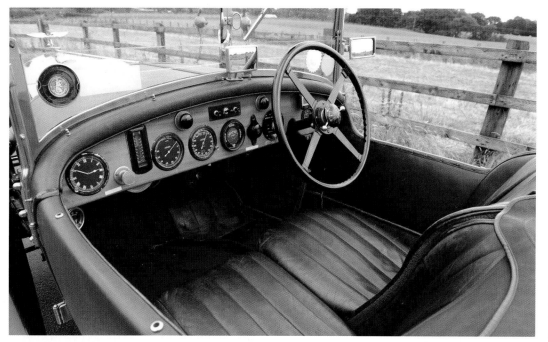

Another innovation for the 1928 season was a spring-spoke steering wheel, which did not meet with universal enthusiasm. Compare this with the solid-spoke wheel of the 3-litre picture on page 40. As before, the throttle adjustment levers were on either side of the steering wheel boss.

The radiator badge of the 4½-litre had a black background. The capital B was originally in white enamel, but in this case most of the enamel has worn off over the years.

Most revealing, perhaps, is that these qualities seemed not to diminish with age and use, testimony to the underlying quality of the car's manufacture. In its issue dated 7 April 1933, *The Autocar* tested a four-year old Weymann four-light saloon with body by Mann Egerton that had then come onto the used car market. It was a March 1929 car, on chassis number AB3354, and by then had 30,000 miles of use behind it. (The car still survives, although like so many other saloons of the time it now has a replica Vanden Plas tourer body.) Weymann bodies were not noted for their longevity, and in this case "one or two rattles were noticeable in the coachwork, which, however, had been well cared for and was almost unmarked".

What stood out, though, was the performance. *The Autocar* was unable to better 78mph, but believed 85mph should be possible. (For comparison, *The Motor* had achieved 90mph with its Vanden Plas tourer-bodied test car in 1928, and *The Autocar* claimed 93mph in 1929 for a similarly-bodied car.) Even so, "a comfortable cruising speed of 60mph up hill and down dale... made for high averages on a long run" and "the power developed by the four-cylinder engine, combined with the general feeling of sturdiness, seemed to give the car complete and easy mastery over other machines met within a run." Despite a specification which had looked old-fashioned in 1929, the 4½-litre was still a machine to be reckoned with in 1933.

At first sight, the 4½-litre engine looks very similar to the older 3-litre – and indeed, it was. There were many important differences, however. The carburettors here are again "sloper" SUs, but very apparent is the large Ki-gass injector above the steering column, added to improve starting. This car has been fitted with a modern Kenlowe electric fan to prevent overheating difficulties in heavy traffic.

In the first few months of 1928, more powerful ER4 magnetos were fitted in place of the original GR4s, to help tackle a starting problem.

Clear in this picture is the forward mounting of the strut gear used on all the long-chassis cars.

Just enough room, and no more! The cockpit of the Vanden Plas tourer body seems snug when the tonneau cover is over the rear seats. There's a fine array of instruments, neatly arranged on the dashboard. The temperature gauge below the dash on the passengers side is a modern precautionary addition.

Instruments on this 4½-litre included a speedometer marked to 120mph, rather than the 100mph of the 3-litre.

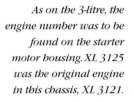

As on the 3-litre, the engine number was to be found on the starter motor housing. XL 3125 was the original engine in this chassis, XL 3121.

As on earlier Bentleys, the chassis number of the 4½-litre could be found at the base of the steering column.

Some cars had a fixed starting handle, but on others it was removable. This stowage solution is seen on the 4½-litre engine of AB 3351, a slightly later car delivered in November 1928.

Chapter Six

The Supercharged 4½-Litres

There's a rather splendid irony in the fact that the general public's enduring vision of a vintage Bentley is a supercharged 4½-litre model with a Vanden Plas open four-seater body painted in the dark green used on Bentley team cars. There certainly were many such cars, but they were hardly typical of the marque. The supercharged 4½-litre model was in fact what we would now call a "homologation special", built in small numbers to enable an ultra-high-performance derivative to meet racing regulations which required that a certain number of production cars had been or would be built.

WO Bentley himself in fact disapproved quite strongly of the supercharged cars. As he wrote in *An Illustrated History of the Bentley Car*: "I never much liked them; to increase performance, I always preferred the idea of making the engine bigger… The part I liked least was having to make fifty of them and offer them for sale in order that they could enter for Le Mans. This diverted a lot of our resources and materials, but Barnato liked the idea, and he held the purse-strings." Even more memorably, he wrote in his autobiography that "To supercharge the Bentley engine was to pervert its design and corrupt its performance."

So how did the supercharged Bentley ever come about? It came about as a direct result of the Bentley racing programme. As the 1928 season wore on, it was becoming increasingly apparent that the 4½-litre car was up against some fierce opposition. The latest Alfa Romeos were snapping at its heels, the Bugattis were formidable opponents, and of course the big Mercedes SS cars with their 7.1-litre engines were already employing superchargers – albeit to supply transient rather than constant boosts of power.

WO Bentley was well aware of this, and he believed that a racing derivative of the new 6½-litre six-cylinder engine would restore Bentley supremacy. That engine materialised in due course as the engine of the Speed Six in 1929 and went on to deliver Bentley victories in competition with the marque's customary reliability. However, from within the heart of the Bentley Boys themselves came a voice of dissent, or perhaps of impatience. That voice was the voice of Tim Birkin. An intensely patriotic man, he was genuinely concerned to see British cars leading the field in international events. In the 1928 German Grand Prix at the Nurburgring, he was deeply disappointed to finish in eighth place with his 4½-litre Bentley. Ahead of him were three Bugattis – light racing machines – and four Mercedes. All had supercharged engines.

The Bugattis – Type 35 machines – were small and light, but the Mercedes was a car of broadly similar dimensions to the Bentley, sitting on a 3400mm (134-inch) wheelbase. Its engine was a 7065cc six-cylinder which developed around 170bhp – already significantly more than the 130bhp of a Le Mans-specification Bentley 4½-

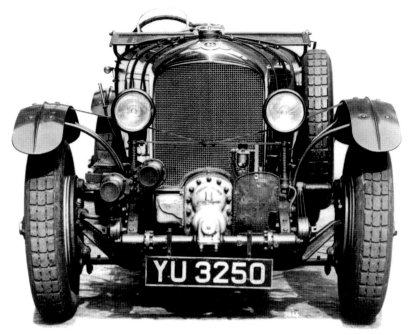

*The first supercharged Bentley started
life as an ordinary 4½-litre owned by
Bentley team driver Bernard Rubin. It
was rebuilt on a new chassis frame and
re-numbered HB3404 within the
sequence allocated to Tim Birkin's
workshop; then, when somebody
discovered that the number HB3404
had already been allocated elsewhere, it
became HB3404/R. Clearly visible in
this picture is the supercharger between
the front dumb-irons. On its casing can
be seen the cast lettering that marked
the design as belonging to Amherst
Villiers. The carburettors are protected
by the mesh screen visible on the right
of the radiator here.*

litre. But, critically, it had a Roots-type super-charger which would boost engine power to around 225bhp in short bursts. In the hands of a skilled and determined driver like Rudolf Carac-ciola, the star of the Mercedes team, it was virtually unbeatable. Mercedes had been using supercharged engines since 1923, and were clearly going to continue using this new and fashionable technology, which had its origins in aircraft engines. Birkin felt that this was the way Bentley should also go if it was to remain successful in international competition.

So he decided to talk to the acknowledged British expert on supercharging, an engineer called Amherst Villiers who had set himself up in London as a consultant on supercharging to the motor industry. Villiers had an impressive track record. He had worked with Raymond Mays, helping the racing driver get the most from his Brescia Bugattis and fitting a Roots-type supercharger to his 1922 Vauxhall TT car to produce the Vauxhall Villiers Supercharged Special. Most recently, he had worked with Malcolm Campbell, designing the Bluebird car with which Campbell took the World Land Speed Record on Pendine Sands in February 1927. This was clearly the man Birkin needed, and the Bentley driver asked him to look at supercharging a 4½-litre Bentley engine.

Villiers started work in the late autumn of 1928. At an early stage, he called for the blue-prints of the Bentley engine, which of course could not be obtained without WO Bentley's

Under the skin of the supercharged Bentley: this picture was taken when the late Harry Rose was rebuilding the car. Note the special front tie-bar supporting the nose of the supercharger, which by this stage had a replacement casing. Also visible is the trunking leading from the supercharger to the engine's inlet manifold.

LE MANS RECORD LAP CAR 1930 DRIVEN BY SIR H.R.S. BIRKIN. BT.

This cutaway drawing of a Birkin "blower" – notionally at least HB3403, with which Birkin took the lap record at Le Mans in 1930 – shows the overall layout of the cars. The blow-off valves are visible alongside the inlet manifold, where the carburettors would be on an unblown 4½-litre engine. The body is of course the ubiquitous Vanden Plas sports four-seater, in this case with cycle wings.

consent. WO appears to have been reluctant from the start, but Birkin enlisted the support of Barnato. WO could hardly refuse when the man who was funding his company insisted.

So, no doubt giving in gracefully but with considerable doubts in his mind, WO discussed the task with Villiers. The latter could see quite clearly that the existing engine needed to be quite considerably strengthened to withstand the additional stresses that the supercharger would impose. His plan was to use a Roots-type supercharger that would be permanently engaged; this was quite different from the Mercedes system where the supercharger was engaged by means of a clutch when extra power was needed for overtaking.

Villiers wanted a larger-diameter crankshaft and he wanted it counter-balanced to give smooth running. He wanted larger-diameter main bearings, which in turn demanded modifications to the lower end of the cylinder block. He wanted a stiffer crankcase, and of course the engine would need stronger pistons and

connecting rods; in practice, they would have stronger gudgeon pins as well. WO accepted all these recommendations with the exception of the counter-balanced crankshaft. Instead, he wanted the crankshaft to rely on additional size. Villiers accepted the compromise, but it was a compromise that did nothing for the reliability of the supercharged engine. The so-called "heavy crank" was prone to an out-of-balance vibration that tended to destroy the centre main bearing if the car was driven hard – as its specification inevitably invited.

There was also the issue of where to mount the supercharger. WO believed in driving engine ancillaries through gears, and mistrusted belts and chains which were more prone to failures. So he suggested that the supercharger should be mounted ahead of the radiator between the chassis dumb-irons, in much the same way as had been done for the dynamo on the six-cylinder Bentleys. Here, it would be driven from the front of the crankshaft, the drive being taken through a fabric joint to the rearmost of the two rotors and by means of a gear train to the forward rotor. Lubrication would be direct, by a take-off from the engine's own oil system but with its own pump. A scavenger pump would collect surplus oil and return it to the crankcase. A special inlet manifold would also be needed, incorporating a pair of blow-off valves to prevent backfiring through the supercharger. On production cars, there was a third blow-off valve on the underside of the exhaust system.

Agreement was reached in October 1928. Bentley Motors had to build a minimum of 50 "production" cars to enable the supercharged 4½-litre to race at Le Mans, and the deal gave the company cost-free use of the Villiers design until May 1929. Birkin was paying Villiers to do the design independently of Bentley Motors. If Bentley chose to continue building supercharged cars after that date, they would pay Villiers a royalty.

Birkin's plan was to press ahead with the development of the new supercharged car with all speed. He was so convinced that it would be a success that among his first actions was to enter a team of two supercharged Bentleys for the 1929 Le Mans event, scheduled for 15 and 16 June. That gave barely nine months to complete the design, test a prototype, and build the race cars. As Bentley Motors was in no position to do so, and WO himself was not keen enough on the idea to make room for it in his company's programme, Birkin invested his own money in the scheme.

He established a workshop at Welwyn Garden City, a new town established in 1920 in the Hertfordshire countryside. The choice was largely dictated by its reasonable proximity to Bentley Motors at Cricklewood. To run the supercharged project, Birkin engaged Clive Gallop, another former Royal Flying Corps officer who was more than a little familiar with Bentley cars. He had designed the four-valves-per-cylinder camshaft of the original 3-litre engine back in 1919, and in 1926 he had prepared "Scrap" Thistlethwayte's 3-litre for Le Mans, joining him in the car as riding mechanic and co-driver.

Gallop was probably the ideal man for the job, but there was one problem. He and Amherst Villiers did not get on, and differences between them eventually led to Villiers walking away from the project. Nevertheless, Villiers

played his part. Birkin had persuaded fellow Bentley Boy Bernard Rubin to allow his own 4½-litre to be used as the prototype, and to this Villiers fitted the first "blower" installation. (The car was on chassis number HF3187, but was given a new 10ft 10in chassis frame along with its supercharged engine and re-numbered as HB3404/R. The R suffix was added when somebody later discovered that this number had also allocated to another "blower" Bentley which had been bodied as a saloon by HJ Mulliner. It stood for either Rubin, the former owner of the car, or Rebuilt, depending on whose account you read.)

The first design of supercharger consisted of twin rotors inside an aluminium casing which was partially double-walled. Into this casing, as agreed with WO in October 1928, were cast raised letters that read, "Amherst Villiers Supercharger Mk IV", and a second small plate attached to the casing bore the Villiers logo. The supercharger drew fuel-air mixture from the two Zenith carburettors mounted rather vulnerably on its left-hand side, between the chassis dumb-irons, and forced it upwards at between 10 and 11psi through trunking leading to the inlet manifold on the right.

There was no doubt about the success of the principle. In later production form, when twin SU carburettors were used, the Le Mans-specification Birkin "blower" engine delivered 240bhp at 4200rpm – a truly massive increase over the 130bhp of a Le Mans-specification unblown 4½-litre. However, Birkin was not quite there yet. The casing of the initial supercharger did not expand uniformly as it heated up because it was only partially double-walled; it distorted, which in turn caused it to foul the rotors. So Villiers redesigned it with a more uniform single-wall

This picture from the Welwyn Garden City workshop was obviously posed, but seems to show one of the Birkin "blowers" under construction in 1928. The machine-turned dashboard is clearly visible, as is the large rev-counter used on the racing cars.

The "production" supercharged chassis were taken to the Brooklands track to be tested. This is a car from the second batch of 25, with the ribbed supercharger casing. The twin spare wheels are providing a certain amount of ballast, and there are rudimentary bucket seats for the occupants.

casing incorporating cooling fins. It was more or less his last input to the Birkin Bentley project before he quit.

Meanwhile, Bentley Motors had supplied Birkin's Welwyn Garden City workshop with two 4½-litre chassis. These were to be turned into the Le Mans race cars. They were bodied by Harrison's as four-seater tourers, constructed using the British Flexible body patents. The first of them, always known as the No1 car even though the prototype car had preceded it, was running just a few days before Le Mans in June 1929.

It was, though, too late. On test at Brooklands, the supercharged car revealed oil pressure problems and endless trouble with oiled plugs. These were evidently not going to be solved in a hurry, so Birkin reluctantly withdrew his cars from Le Mans. Bentley Motors stepped in by providing two replacement 4½-litre cars, and put Birkin into a Speed Six alongside Barnato. The Speed Six finished first; one 4½-litre did not finish the race; but second, third and fourth places all went to 4½-litre "works" Bentleys. Clearly, there was still life in the car that Birkin had been ready to write off a year earlier.

Meanwhile, Bentley had also begun production of their first batch of supercharged chassis. These clearly did not meet with the approval of the Cricklewood workforce, as Elizabeth Nagle discovered when preparing her book, *The Other Bentley Boys*. Nobby Clarke, Bentley's long-

serving Service Foreman, was quite forthright on the subject: "The trouble with the superchargers was that we knew nothing about them at that time. Nothing about the effect of pressures, or the effect of overloading – all the problems related to them. We'd no idea how they would behave; we were only on the fringe of knowing something about blowers, and the results proved it. I was against the idea right from the start... The supercharger was no good at variable speeds – for ordinary road conditions, that is. If it can be run at a constant speed the whole time – flat out, or nearly flat out – then it works. But there's still the overheating problem. No, those superchargers were a very bad idea, and they did us a lot of harm."

This opinion was shared by Wally Hassan, who at the time of the "blowers" was a travelling service specialist and an integral part of the "works" team. "It was an unsatisfactory thing, that supercharger – huge, bigger than the gearbox – it outbalanced the car, I thought, and it never really worked. And it did the firm no good – harm, really. Those that were raced weren't Works cars, but the public thought they were; and, of course, they wasted money."

The supercharged Bentley was announced to the public in *The Autocar* of 5 July 1929 and was officially introduced at the Paris Motor Show that autumn. But both of these events were pre-production publicity, because no chassis were actually ready in time for the Paris Show. By the time of the "home" show at Olympia in October, though, two chassis had not only been completed but also bodied. Bentley Motors showed, somewhat predictably, an open Vanden Plas sports model, which later became their demonstrator. This was on chassis SM3903, the first production example. Meanwhile, Freestone & Webb had a fixed-head coupé of their own design on their stand. At £1475, the chassis was considerably more expensive than the standard 4½-litre at £1050, but it was also a lot cheaper than the Speed Six at £1800.

It was only to be expected that the production engines would be rather less powerful than the Le Mans-tune engines that came from the Birkin workshop, but with 175bhp they were still hugely more powerful than the 110bhp unblown standard engines. Their superchargers delivered a lower boost of 9.5psi at 3500rpm and 10psi at 3900rpm, and they had a lower compression ratio as well. Both changes were probably made in the interests of reliability.

As so often happened in the Bentley story, things did not run entirely smoothly. Amherst Villiers visited the Olympia show on its first day, and was somewhat taken aback to discover that his name had disappeared from the casing of the Bentley's supercharger. He complained, and that evening Bentley Motors' head storeman Conway was despatched to Olympia with Villiers badges and instructed to fit them to the show cars. The new sales catalogue was also hastily withdrawn for an amendment, which was made in such a hurry that the reference to the Amherst Villiers Mk IV supercharger was misaligned on the page.

Villiers did not let it rest there and sued Bentley Motors, claiming £1000 damages. He walked away from the court case with £100 and the promise of the rest at a later date, but he never did receive his £900. Bentley Motors went under before they could pay him. In a further irony, the Villiers badge that did get fitted to production cars was usually concealed under a cowling over the supercharger.

The 50 supercharged cars built by Bentley Motors were constructed in two batches of 25, it being company policy at the time to sanction production in batches of this size. The second batch of cars (the MS series) had a ribbed supercharger casing, which made them easy to distinguish from the first batch (the SM series) which had a plain supercharger casing. The supercharger installation demanded a special chassis front cross-member and tie-bar, plus a radiator with its bottom cut away and a thicker core to compensate for this loss. All cars were originally fitted with the D-type gearbox, Woodhead front and Berry rear springs, and André dampers. The magnetos were by Bosch, type FF4 or FV4B, and there were twin Autopulse

On the production cars, the supercharger was usually concealed behind a protective fairing, as seen here. This car was on chassis number SM3918, and was specially built for Birkin's friend Billy Fiske, an American-born multi-millionaire socialite living in Paris. It had the full Birkin team-car specification, with Vanden Plas four-seat body on a split-pinned chassis fitted with the long bonnet and 42-gallon fuel tank. It also had a Le Mans dashboard, inboard adjustable brakes and onboard oil tank as well as a quick-release hood and windscreen.

electric fuel pumps. Towards the end of the second batch, at chassis MS3941, a 25-gallon fuel tank was standardised in place of the earlier 16-gallon type: the blower Bentley could be thirsty in the hands of a driver who enjoyed using it to the full.

More than half of the 50 "production" supercharged models were completed as Vanden Plas open four-seaters in the image of the Bentley team cars, which was perhaps no big surprise. After all, the sales brochure, which was actually an addendum to the catalogue for the standard 4½-litre, had pointed out that "the appeal of the new type will be to the super-sporting enthusiast whose delight it is to possess just that 'little bit extra'." Since the car looked like one of the successful Le Mans racers and could out-accelerate almost anything else on the road in 1929, it most certainly fitted that description.

Many of the supercharged cars were fitted with the longer bonnet of the six-cylinder models, which aided the visual impression of

power that owners understandably wanted. Only a handful of the 50 production chassis had closed bodies – six or seven, according to the best authorities – and all those have since either disappeared or been replaced by modern replica tourer types. Vanden Plas built the bodies on no fewer than 34 of the production cars, and when London dealer Jack Barclay bought the last eight chassis after Bentley Motors had gone into receivership, he had seven of them bodied as Vanden Plas drophead coupés.

There is one school of thought which has it that Bentley Motors would have switched production of their 4½-litre model over entirely to the supercharged version if it had been successful. From late 1929, all 4½-litre engines were built with the heavier crankcase designed for the supercharged engine, and adherents of the "changeover" theory point to this as proof that the intention was to build only supercharged engines at some point in the near future. Against this we can quote the intention recorded in *The Motor* for 5 July 1929, which may or not be fully representative of the truth: "It is not really intended that the supercharged machine shall supersede the earlier model in any way whatever."

There is also an alternative and probably equally plausible explanation, namely that it was quite simply cheaper to standardise a common crankcase (and other components) in

production when the heavier crankcase was needed for the production batch of supercharged cars. Bentley Motors was, as always, short of cash: having two different crankcases and crankshafts (etcetera) in production at the same time was more expensive than having a single design that could be made to suit both supercharged and unsupercharged engines. So the components needed for the supercharged engines were standardised for the unsupercharged ones as far as possible. If nothing else, this arrangement at least gave the flexibility that production in the longer term could switch to all supercharged cars, all unsupercharged, or a mixture of the two. Everything depended on how the customers took to the supercharged version.

We now know that the supercharged 4½-litre was not really a commercial success. As Michael Hay put it so memorably in *Bentley 4½-litre Supercharged*: "Customers simply did not line up to pay large amounts of money for what was basically a 1919 design, itself based on 1914 concepts, updated and redesigned." *Motor Sport* for January 1931 was a little more charitable, arguing that some prospective buyers had held back from buying supercharged Bentleys when they were first introduced, wanting to see first how they would perform in their first season of racing. That may or may not be true: the motoring press tended to pull punches quite a lot at the time.

This was SM3907 when new in June 1930, complete with the stylish wheel discs which became popular in the late 1920s and disguised the standard wire wheels. The body is of course a Vanden Plas four-seater, with fabric panelling.

One way or another, it had also been a bad time to launch any new and expensive car. October 1929, the month when the supercharged 4½-litre was announced to the public, was also the month of the Wall Street Crash. This in turn triggered the Great Depression, in which many of the traditionally rich suddenly found themselves not so rich any more and either no longer willing or no longer able to spend money on such luxuries as fast cars. The supercharged 4½-litre undoubtedly suffered as a result – as indeed did the whole of Bentley Motors.

At the Olympia Show in 1930, the Bentley Motors stand had a high-sided tourer on the supercharged chassis, and a second supercharged chassis was shown on the Vanden Plas stand with that company's own fixed-head coupé bodywork. But the cars were still not selling well. In January 1931, the chassis price was dropped dramatically to £1150 – a 22% reduction over the original price, which Bentley must have hoped would help move their remaining stock of supercharged chassis. Yet buyers did not flock to hand over their cheques. When Bentley Motors went into receivership in July 1931 there was still a stock of unsold supercharged 4½-litre chassis, and the last cars were not sold until well into 1932.

As for Tim Birkin, Chapter 9 shows how he campaigned his "blowers" with relentless enthusiasm and determination, but ultimately without the success he wanted. In the beginning, he had built four cars at Welwyn Garden City, one of them rebuilt from Bernard Rubin's unsupercharged 4½-litre. All had been numbered in a sequence allocated by Bentley Motors for Birkin to use. But once the Hon Dorothy Paget cut off his funding at the end of 1930, Birkin's operation became as starved of funds as Bentley Motors were at the time. He built a fifth supercharged car from spares, and gave it another chassis number from the batch allocated to him, but his aim was probably to generate some cash and the car was sold off very soon afterwards. The remaining Birkin team cars were advertised for sale in *Motor Sport* for May 1931 to raise money, and Birkin himself entered into an ill-fated partnership with racing driver Mike Couper, devoting his workshop to the preparation of racing cars for other people.

Looking back, it is undeniable that the "blower" Bentley was a failure – but equally undeniable is that it was an heroic failure. It never achieved in competition what its originator wanted for it, constantly suffering from overheating and lubrication problems, and regularly oiling its plugs unless carefully treated.

The overheating resulted mainly from the location of the supercharger: it reduced the frontal surface of the radiator, and as a result the supercharged cars had a coolant capacity of just 5 gallons instead of the 5¾ gallons of the standard 4½-litre cars. The supercharger also

This gorgeous body was the work of Gurney Nutting, and was built to order for Woolf Barnato, then the Chairman of Bentley motors. It was on supercharged chassis SM3909. A similar style, but this time built as a fixed-head coupé, was used for the Speed Six with which Barnato supposedly raced the famous Blue Train in March 1930 – although it is now clear that the car he used was actually a less glamorous Mulliner saloon.

reduced airflow over the sump, resulting in higher oil temperatures. And, of course, the supercharger placed additional stresses on the engine, which in turn generated more heat.

The lubrication problems were eventually solved when the Birkin single-seater was converted to dry-sump lubrication in the 1930s. By then, however, it was too late to matter. As for plug-oiling, this was less of a problem in competition than in road use. Long experience with the model enabled the Bentley Drivers' Club to warn many years later in *The Technical Facts of the Vintage Bentley* that the engine should never be allowed to idle but should always be run at 1000rpm or more. There was, too, a complicated recommendation for clearing fouled plugs if the inevitable happened.

Most tellingly, perhaps, WO Bentley was proved right in the end, although he was too much of a gentleman ever to say so. He never did believe in the supercharged cars, insisting that a racing derivative of his six-cylinder 6½-litre engine would do all that was necessary. The "works" Speed Sixes so often did better than the Birkin supercharged cars when the two entered the same races that there was no need for him to press his point.

Yet it would be wrong to undervalue Birkin's achievement with the supercharged cars. He developed some exceptionally quick racing machines, and even WO was moved to add rather admiringly in *An Illustrated History of the*

Bentley Car that, "of course, they were very fast while they lasted". Their biggest failing was unreliability – and that was something that went against everything WO held dear.

DRIVING THE SUPERCHARGED BENTLEY

The motoring press did not get their hands on a supercharged car until the spring of 1930, although – as noted earlier – *The Motor* had announced its impending arrival in July 1929. It was again *The Motor* which led the field, testing the Vanden Plas-bodied UW 3761 (chassis SM3903, the Olympia Motor Show car) for its issue dated 22 April 1930. For what it is worth, they gave top speed as 103mph and 0-60mph acceleration as a curiously slow 20 seconds, while fuel consumption was 12mpg at high average speeds. However, while the acceleration

4½-LITRE SUPERCHARGED BENTLEY PRODUCTION			
Note: These figures are taken from Bentley Drivers' Club records. They relate to "season" and not to calendar year.			
	Birkin cars	**Cricklewood cars**	**Total**
1929	3		3
1930	2	13	15
1931		37	37
Total	**5**	**50**	**55**

and top speed of the car impressed them when they tested the car at Brooklands, more impressive still was the smoothness and flexibility of its engine. It was, they said, "far more smooth and more flexible than a car with a big four-cylinder engine has any right to be!... it can chug along quite quietly and comfortably at less than 10mph on its top-gear ratio of 3½ to 1. Considering that the maximum speed on the same gear is well over 100mph, this represents a remarkable achievement".

The engine was not noisy, either, being "particularly quiet for a sports job, the silencing being as effective as anyone could desire". Nor was the supercharger intrusive, "just a faint whisper being heard when running with the throttle almost shut at less than 30mph". The brakes were excellent, and the figures achieved "were so good as to make us re-check lest a mistake should have occurred!" Even the suspension came in for only mild criticism, as it was "on the harsh side, but... not uncomfortable". Overall, the supercharged car was "a delight to drive, holding the road like a leech and enabling one to take advantage of gaps in heavy traffic without inconveniencing anyone, so quickly is the obstruction cleared".

The Autocar road-tested GH 3951 (chassis number SM3917) in its issue of 19 September 1930, and described it as "a car with the strongest possible individuality... immensely likeable". The article's sub-title – "the appeal of

immense power, linked with great docility" – again stressed the supercharged Bentley's untemperamental behaviour despite its high performance. That the engine delivered huge power was beyond doubt: "There is so much power that even on a high top ratio the majority of hills can be taken fast". And once again the refinement of the supercharger installation occasioned comment:

"There is practically nothing which makes the car any different to handle from any other

> *Another legendary supercharged Bentley was the Birkin single-seater, on chassis HB3402. Originally built with an open four-seater body by Harrison, the car was completely rebuilt over the winter of 1929-30 with a streamlined single-seater body and was campaigned by Birkin personally.*

CHASSIS NUMBERS OF THE SUPERCHARGED 4½-LITRE CARS

The Birkin cars
HB3402 and HB3403 were the "No 1" and "No 2" cars
HB3404/R was the prototype and the "No 3" car; it was built as a standard 4½-litre chassis HF3187 and was re-numbered
HR3976 and HR3977 were built from parts in 1930

The production cars
1930 chassis	SM3901-SM3913
1931 chassis	SM3914-SM3925
	MS3926-MS3950

SPECIFICATIONS FOR BENTLEY 4½-LITRE SUPERCHARGED MODELS

Years of manufacture
1929
Build quantity
55 (50 "factory" cars and 5 "Birkin" cars)

Engine
4398cc (100mm x 140mm)
OHC monobloc four-cylinder with four valves and two spark plugs per cylinder
Amherst Villiers MkIV Roots-type supercharger delivering 9.5lb boost at 3500rpm
and 10lb boost at 3900rpm (up to 12lb boost on Birkin cars)
Two SU HVG 5 carburettors
4.5:1 compression ratio (with compression plate)
5.1:1 compression ratio (Birkin Le Mans specification)
175bhp at 3500 rpm (4.5:1 compression) or 182bhp at 3900rpm (5.1:1 compression)

Transmission
Four-speed D-type "crash" gearbox:
2.64:1, 1.63:1, 1.35:1, 1.00:1, reverse 2.64:1
Single dry plate clutch
Final drive ratio: Standard 3.53:1
                   Special order 3.3:1
Four-star Speed Six pattern differential

Axles and suspension
Front: H-section beam axle; some cars with integral jacking lugs
Woodhead semi-elliptic leaf springs (leaf numbers dependent on body weight)
André shock absorbers
Rear: Welded pressed steel casing with semi-floating half-shafts
Berry semi-elliptic leaf springs (leaf numbers dependent on body weight)
André shock absorbers

Steering
Worm and wheel steering with 10.3:1 ratio

Brakes
Rudge-Whitworth centre-lock wire wheels with Dunlop 6.00 x 21 well-base tyres

Chassis dimensions

Wheelbase:	10ft 10in
Overall length:	14ft 4½in
Overall width:	5ft 8½in
Track:	56in front and rear
Weight:	28.5cwt

Performance

Max. speed:	103mph
0-60mph:	13.5 secs approx

machine: certainly there is no suggestion of fierceness… from inside the car the sound of the supercharger itself is scarcely audible."

When *Motor Sport* tested SM3903 for their January 1931 issue, they too were impressed by its "refined and effortless performance", pointing out that it was "more docile at really low engine speeds than the standard 4½-litre model". However, the performance occasioned this comment: "The supercharging has also made possible remarkable acceleration, and when a stretch of open road appears, and the gears are used as they should be, the car momentarily doffs its sheep's clothing and reveals its ancestry of well-tried racers."

In addition, "The production model is a genuine hundred-mile-and-hour car, and as such it takes its place without question among the élite of the world's sporting cars. It is, however, more in the manner in which it accomplishes things, rather than in the bald figures themselves, that the true character of the car becomes apparent." Other characteristics were the light and sensitive steering, the "extremely powerful" brakes, and the "steadiness at all speeds". This was "A car for the connoisseur of sporting cars, and moreover, proof that this country can still make a car which can compete with confidence and success with the best the world produces."

Yet it is interesting to see how *The Autocar* reacted to a supercharged Bentley when testing

one for its issue of 20 July 1934, some time after production had ended. The car itself was chassis number MS 3942, registered in December 1931, and it was borrowed from HM Bentley and Partners, who had carried out some of their characteristic modifications. It went extremely well: "Its principal appeal lies in the extraordinary ease with which the machine gets over the ground at speeds which are the all-out limit of most machines." The downside was that it needed acclimatisation. "The gear change needed knowing, in view of the close ratios", and "Until one became accustomed to the car, if the throttle were treated carelessly there was sometimes a loud explosion and smoke from the supercharger blow-off valves."

Although originally on a 10ft 10in wheelbase chassis and bodied by Harrison, HB 3403 was cut down to a 9ft 9½in wheelbase in 1930 and rebodied by Vanden Plas. It is now in the collection of Bentley Motors. Birkin drove this car at Le Mans in 1930. The additional bonnet louvres were designed to help keep the supercharged engine cool.

The radiator badge was the same as that of the standard 4½-litre. As a Le Mans car, this example has a quick-release radiator filler.

Le Mans necessities included the huge fuel tank with quick-action filler cap visible in these shots of the supercharged car. The car raced as number 9 at Le Mans in 1930 (see Chapter 9), and still retains the race markings for that event.

The twin SU carburettors can be seen here alongside the supercharger that was driven from the nose of the crankshaft. This was a race-prepared engine, and so there is a profusion of split-pinned bolts and wired nuts which would not have been found on a production supercharged car. That is a horn underneath the headlamp – moved to the front of the car where it would be most effective at Le Mans.

The inlet side of the supercharged engine is quite different from that of a standard production 4½-litre. There are no carburettors; instead, there is massive trunking leading downwards and then forward to the supercharger, while a pair of huge blow-off valves protect the supercharger from the effects of a backfire. Additional linkages and cross-shafts were needed to connect to the carburettors, now located out front next to the supercharger.

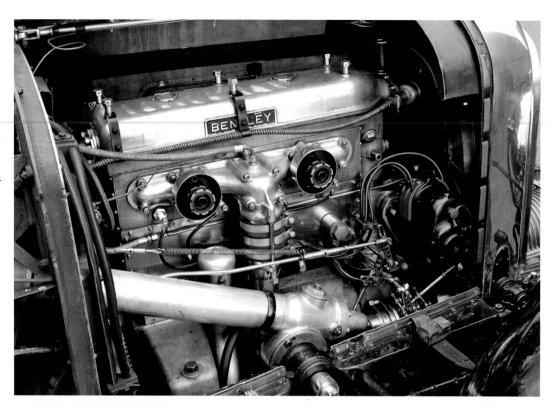

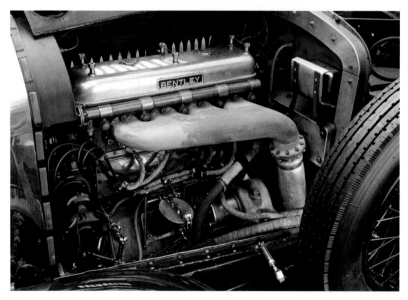

Interesting on the exhaust side of the engine is the asbestos lagging on the HT leads, applied to all the supercharged cars because of the additional heat generated by the engine.

This race-prepared engine has a quick-release oil filler cap; ordinary production cars had one with a cut-out B like that seen on other Bentley engines.

Old Bentleys just get faster: the final entry on this plaque commemorating its racing history dates from 1959, when it achieved a flying mile of over 125mph in the hands of Stanley Sears on the Jabbeke highway near Antwerp.

Very much not to production standard was the dashboard created for the racing Blowers by Tim Birkin. Rather than wood, it is made of hand-turned aluminium, and carries a profusion of instruments and switches that were simply not needed on production cars. The dominant instrument is a huge rev counter, redlined at 4500rpm. The speedometer, which reads to 140mph, is tucked away in the corner on the passenger's side.

Chapter Seven

Coachwork on 4½-Litre and 4½-Litre Supercharged Cars

There were far fewer "standard" designs for the 4½-litre Bentley and for the super-charged version than there had been for the 3-litre chassis. To a large extent, this probably reflected the fact that the carriage trade was now focussing on the 6½-litre six-cylinder chassis for formal bodywork; the fact that the famous "bloody thump" of the 4½-litre engine made it difficult to design a closed body with adequate levels of refinement probably explained the rest. Even so, there was no lack of variety among the bespoke bodies that customers ordered.

Sporting Four-seaters

The standard Sporting Four-seater on the 4½-

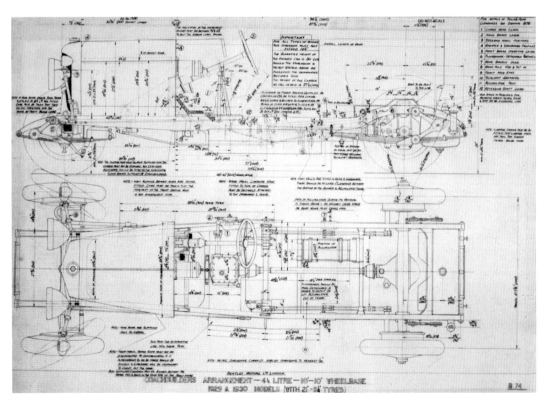

From the Bentley Drivers' Club archive comes this picture of a Coachbuilder's Arrangement drawing for the 1929-1930 4½-litre chassis. Provided by Bentley Motors, it enabled draughtsmen working for a coachbuilder to draw up their own "blueprint" for a body design.

From Vanden Plas's own records comes this picture of a Sporting Four-seater to the standard style on the 4½-litre chassis.

Not every Sporting Four-seater looked the same, thanks to variations in such things as headlamp style and the design of the wings. However, the basic body design dated from 3-litre days, and was represented like this in the April 1928 sales catalogue.

litre chassis was already familiar to buyers of the 3-litre. Vanden Plas provided its characteristic design with outside handbrake and asymmetric door arrangement. The price was the same throughout, at £1295. There was, as always, room for individual variation in such things as the style of running-boards and the lighting arrangements. Some later examples had the cycle-type wings then favoured by the sporting fraternity, together with such items as side steps in place of running-boards, and louvred chassis valances.

At Olympia in 1927, the Bentley Motors stand displayed a 4½-litre (chassis number ST3006) with this body style in black with red interior and aluminium-finish wings. Then, in 1928, Vanden Plas showed another (on chassis number XR3335) on their own stand incorporating the fairly popular option of the bonnet panels from a 6½-litre: with an extra seven inches of length as compared to the standard four-cylinder type, they gave a pleasing impression of power and speed.

There was at least one demonstrator with the open four-seater body. This was KL3578 from October 1929, which was later sold to speed ace Sir Malcolm Campbell. There was another Show example, too. This was on chassis number XF3517 from September 1929 and appeared on the Bentley Motors stand at the Paris Show that year, the one and only time the marque appeared there during its Cricklewood days.

This is 4½-litre chassis HF 3185, from May 1928, with all-weather body by H J Mulliner.

Sporting Two-seaters

A Sporting Two-seater model did not appear in the 4½-litre catalogue until April 1928, and was then not listed again after October 1928. It was once again a Vanden Plas design, their number 362 which they knew as the Standard Open Two-Seater, and had a two-seat dickey in addition to the main seat, which could be a bench or

The body was able to flex thanks to a layer of felt sandwiched between the two halves of each joint in the framework, while the wood-screws that held the joint were encased in rubber sleeves. Harrison's established British Flexible Coachworks Ltd in 1927 and interestingly, as Nick Walker has pointed out, HM Bentley became a director of this company. By this time, he had of course left Bentley Motors. The British Flexible system did not find many takers, however, and probably the only coachbuilder to use it under licence was Vanden Plas.

Weymann saloons

Weymann saloons were the only enclosed bodies recommended for the 4½-litre chassis, and the standard design was a four-door, four-light type which appeared little different from the Weymann saloons that had been available on the 3-litre chassis. In April 1928, this cost £1495.

"This type of body is built only to order", warned the April 1928 sales catalogue, so customers who wanted an attractive two-seater like this would not be able to buy one from stock. It was a very attractive design, though, and would have been worth waiting for. The panelling was in fabric, and there was a two-seater dickey.

two individual bucket types, either fixed or sliding. "This type of body is only built to order," warned the April 1928 sales catalogue, adding that it could be had with either two spare wheels – in which case they were mounted in the front wings – or one at the rear over the petrol tank. Prices started at £1380.

The Sporting Two-seater body also had fabric rather than metal panels – although the fact that it was not described as being of Weymann construction suggests that it might have incorporated the British Flexible style of construction. This was in effect a way of getting around the Weymann patents which had been developed by Harrison & Sons and was on the market by 1927. It allowed the body to move with the chassis while also allowing the use of metal panelling and therefore more complex curves and gloss paintwork. Fabric panels could of course be used as an alternative.

However, the design did evolve to a degree, and Vanden Plas again did not have things all their own way. Cricklewood took on a four-door Weymann saloon demonstrator by HJ Mulliner on 4½-litre chassis NT3133 in January 1928, and the 1929 Olympia Show car, a four-door, four-light Weymann saloon, was bodied by Gurney Nutting. Its style was known as the "Prince of Wales" type, a name chosen to reflect the then Prince of Wales's choice of Gurney Nutting to body a car for him. It was a style which Gurney Nutting were obviously keen to promote that year because they also built one for a 6½-litre chassis on their own stand. (The Prince of Wales's car was on 4½-litre chassis

The Weymann patents were embodied in this Vanden Plas saloon on the 4½-litre chassis. A black-and-white photograph does not do justice to the original colour scheme, where the main body colour was probably dark blue or maroon, the wings may have been black, and the roof was in a contrasting light-coloured fabric.

BENTLEY AND VANDEN PLAS

One coachbuilder more than any other is associated with the Bentley marque, and that is Vanden Plas. Today, there are more "Vanden Plas" sporting four-seater bodies on Bentley chassis than Vanden Plas themselves ever built. One reason is that replicas of the style are (relatively) affordable, and that the more elaborate closed bodies which have been scrapped in favour of many of these replicas would be hideously expensive to replicate. Another is that many owners, understandably, favour the glamour associated with the open bodywork of the Vanden Plas-built Le Mans cars.

That Vanden Plas had a special relationship with Bentley Motors is undeniable. Both operated from the same area of London, which introduced an element of convenience into the relationship, and it was no real surprise when, for example, Bentley turned to Vanden Plas in 1925 to build a large batch of Light Tourers to a standardised design. Brian Smith explained the relationship in *Vanden Plas, Coachbuilders* like this:

> From very early on Vanden Plas executed a quantity of sub-contract work for Bentleys and in succeeding years these coachbuilders were destined to have a greater share in bodybuilding for Bentleys than any other single concern. The inextricable link had been formed well before 1923 and the events of that year [when Vanden Plas very nearly went under] only served to strengthen the ties. So it came about that with more space than was immediately needed, Vanden Plas offered to lease part of their factory to Bentleys to be used by them for their Service Department... WO Bentley himself was a regular visitor to [the Vanden Plas works at] Kingsbury and he declared that there was nobody in the business who could better Vanden Plas in the building of sports and touring bodies.

Many customers who welcomed guidance from the Bentley sales people about their choice of bodywork must have been steered in the direction of Vanden Plas. It was also Vanden Plas who would build the bodywork for all the Le Mans Bentleys, under WO's personal supervision. But, as Chapter 4 explains, it was not Vanden Plas who initiated the design of the classic sporting four-seater body which today represents so many people's idea of what a vintage Bentley "should" look like.

Different styles of panelling could make a difference to the appearance, too. Although this is again a standard five-seater Vanden Plas open body, it has fabric rather than metal panels. The light-coloured wheels also make their contribution to a more individual appearance.

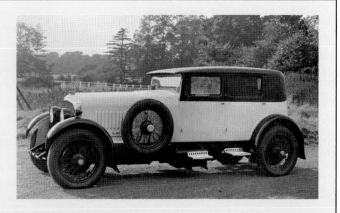

Not a Weymann body this time, although this attractively low-slung style was the work of Vanden Plas. This one was built using the British Flexible patents, and with side-steps and cycle wings in the sporting manner popular in the later 1920s.

The two-tone paintwork in Apple Green and Black would again have made this two-door, four-seat tourer look much more attractive than it does in a black-and-white picture. On chassis number SM3924, it was another elegant Vanden Plas design, and was delivered in January 1931.

This lovely two-tone Weymann saloon was built by Gurney Nutting in May 1928 on chassis number MF3155.

The small rear window does nothing for the looks of this HJ Mulliner saloon on NX3459, but it does make the interior more private for those in the rear seat. The car was delivered in April 1929 and has fabric panelling.

number HB3424 and had cycle wings with a side step rather than running-boards. There were special golf club lockers, smaller than standard side windows, spot lamps operated from the interior, and semaphore indicators.)

By October 1929, the sales catalogue showed a striking Weymann saloon which was very different from what had been available earlier. The windscreen was now raked and the front doors hinged on the centre pillar rather than on the bulkhead. The car pictured was fitted with louvres over the drop-glasses, plus a sun visor over the windscreen and the latest fashion of wheel discs painted to match the bodywork. Both of these latter items – which did make the

car look more modern – cost extra to the advertised price of £1575. The car in the illustration also had cycle-type wings, but no doubt the more traditional style of swept wings and running boards could be had if a customer so wished.

Nevertheless – and despite the insistence in Bentley's sales catalogues that only Weymann construction was suitable for closed bodies – metal-panelled four-door saloons were still in favour. Two such cars were bodied by Freestone & Webb as demonstrators for Bentley Motors. These were XF3150 in January 1930 and FS3614 in October the same year.

Coupés

The coupé design illustrated in the April and October 1928 sales catalogues was none other than HJ Mulliner's Simplex type, with the added benefit of wheel discs which cost extra. Bentley Motors called it a Single Coupé, and it came with fabric panels, a folding top and a two-seater dickey. The basic cost was £1480, and an option for an extra £30 was Triplex glass all round.

By the end of 1928, the HJ Mulliner design was not the only coupé body for the four-cylinder chassis. The coachbuilder Victor Broom, located close to Cricklewood in the NW1 district of London, showed a drophead coupé on chassis number XR3332 at Olympia that year. This was finished in Saxe Blue and Cream, with blue leather upholstery and a

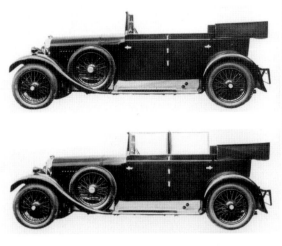

Once again, variations on the "standard" design made for an individual style. This 4½-litre coupé was a Vanden Plas interpretation of the theme. The cycle-type wings and rear-mounted spare give the car a more rakish appearance than the catalogue option from 1928 shown below. The car dates from 1926-27.

All-weather bodies were distinctly old-fashioned by the time Vanden Plas built this one on what is believed to have been PB3548 in July 1930. So calling it by the French name of a Tous Temps type probably helped.

Carlton built the drophead coupé body on DS3562, which was new in August 1929.

The later Single Coupé body design, by HJ Mulliner, is exemplified on this 4½-litre shown as a standard offering in the April 1928 sales catalogue. Once again, the use of wheel discs – which cost extra – made the car look more modern than it would otherwise have done. The body panels were of fabric and the roof folded down. Again, this type of body was built only to order.

Despite the romance that the supercharged chassis promised, buyers did not respond by requesting extravagant or unusual body styles. Though the wings and pontoon-like side steps of this Vanden Plas "special sports tourer" gave it a more streamlined look, the basic body style was pretty much standard for the time. Note the two-tone colour scheme, which would have added hugely to the car's appearance. The supercharger is concealed under a cover panel. This was a late car, on chassis MS3939, and went to Johannesburg.

matching silk headlining for the leather hood. However, it looks as if Victor Broom went out of business after 1929, so there were probably not many more examples of this body style.

The 1930 Olympia Show saw TH Gill & Son, another London coachbuilder from the Paddington area, displaying a third type of coupé body on their own stand. As usual fitted with a dickey seat, this was another drophead type on chassis number FS3620, finished in dark blue and black with a gold coachline and brown leather upholstery. It may have remained unique, as Bentley Motors was by then close to its end.

The Supercharged cars

Reasoning probably that customers for the supercharged 4½-litre were hardy open-air types, Bentley offered only Sporting Four-seater bodywork at first. It was, of course, by Vanden Plas, and it cost a massive £1720 in the lists dated October 1929. This was clearly too much, and by January 1930 the catalogues had been altered to show a price of £1395, which remained in force until the end – although we know from other sources that many supercharged chassis had to be discounted in order to be sold at all.

One supercharged car with open four-seater

Something rather different: this was what Vanden Plas called a "2/3-seater racing body" on the 4½-litre chassis. There seem to have been at least two examples to this style, of which one went to India and the other to Argentina. It looks extraordinary to modern eyes, but would have made a real sporting statement in the late 1920s. It was, of course, too extreme ever to gain the status of a Bentley standard body style!

Again, the supercharged engine did not inspire anything radical in this Weymann-panelled Sportsman's Coupé design by Vanden Plas, but it was nonetheless very attractive. The nose of the supercharger cover panel is just visible.

bodywork appeared on the Bentley Motors stand at Olympia in 1929. This was on chassis number SM3903. Unusually, it was finished in green (perhaps in deliberate reflection of the marque's sporting successes at Le Mans), but with a champagne-coloured interior rather than the black associated with the team cars.

Even though there were customers for the classic Vanden Plas sporting four-seater body right up to the end, the coachbuilder had begun to look ahead. By the time of the supercharged cars, it had developed a very pleasing tourer body with a different and much more modern style. An example was shown on the Bentley Motors stand at Olympia in 1930, and a broadly similar fixed-head coupé on the supercharged

chassis was on that year's Vanden Plas stand. As always, there were variations available to suit individual clients' wishes: cycle-type front wings, for example, could give the design a sporting look, while the alternative of enveloping front wings that swept back into the running-boards produced a more sober and traditional appearance. These bodies were, however, never listed among the standard types in Bentley sales catalogues.

As a last gasp in the January 1931 catalogue, a two-seater body was offered for the supercharged chassis. This was priced at over £1500 and was essentially the same as the Sporting Two-seater that had been available for the unsupercharged 4½-litre during 1928.

As late as January 1931, there was still a market for simple four-seater bodies like this one built by Harrison on chassis number FS3621.

This beautiful 4½-litre illustrates perfectly why questions of originality are such a feature of the vintage Bentley scene. It started life in 1928 as a Freestone & Webb saloon, but was rebuilt onto a reconditioned chassis in 1932. It was also rebodied in the early 1930s by Salmons & Sons with a Tickford folding-head body. Owned by James Medcalf, it is nevertheless one of the most "original" examples surviving today.

The Tickford folding top was a patented design which turned a saloon into an open car but retained the side window frames for weather protection. It was first announced in 1925, and is thus perfectly in keeping with a 1928 Bentley chassis.

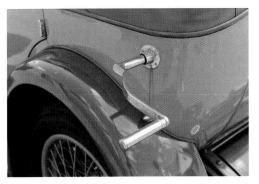

In many ways, the Tickford body was similar to the type then known as an "all-weather". However, it was not a quick or easy task to raise or lower the hood of an all-weather body. The Tickford system demanded minimal effort with a handle, inserted into a geared winding mechanism.

The coachbuilder's plate on this car was attached to the body just below the driver's seat.

The hood was a fairly bulky affair when wound down, but at least the whole of the body was then open to the elements.

The door panels were discreetly finished on this car, with a simple but pleasing sculpted effect on the wood.

The 10ft 10in chassis of the Bentley gave ample rear legroom in a body like this one, and this shot makes clear what the delights of top-down motoring must have been when it was new… on a fine day, of course!

This small flap window recalls the days when the intention to turn was indicated by a clear hand signal rather than by a flashing light. It allowed the main window to remain closed in inclement weather.

With the top up, the Tickford saloon was as weather-proof as any fully panelled saloon of its time.

There never was a standard dashboard for the 4½-litre, although there were some standard items, such as the 110mph speedometer, and the Bentley switchbox. The finished product was therefore down to the taste of the owner and the recommendations of the coachbuilder. In this case, the result was very neat. Note the tidy solution for the outboard handbrake and gear lever, too – although the driver still had to negotiate the levers carefully when getting into or out of the car.

Coachbuilding at its best: discreet touches such as this interior light distinguished the good from the merely mediocre.

Chapter Eight

Motorsport
The 3-Litre Era

The Bentley sporting reputation is based primarily on a string of four consecutive wins at the annual Le Mans 24-hour race between 1927 and 1930. The first three of these wins were by four-cylinder cars, and only the last by a six-cylinder. Yet there was far more depth to the sporting achievements of the Bentley marque than that rapid *résumé* would suggest.

Bentley cars in the 1920s were bought by many gentleman amateurs who enjoyed racing them at weekend club events, and these events kept the Bentley name in the eye of the sporting motorist throughout the decade. The name did not fade with the original company, either, and vintage Bentleys continued to perform well on the track during the 1930s as well. But the club events at which Bentleys raced are of interest now only to the dedicated historian; what mattered most in the 1920s and what still matters most today is the string of international racing successes racked up by the "works" team cars or by cars raced in the Bentley name. Some of those cars also went on to further careers in private hands before it became clear that they were outclassed by more modern machinery.

In fact, the Le Mans event that made the marque's reputation did not even exist when the first Bentleys were built, the first one not being held until 1923. When WO and his colleagues built their cars with the sporting fraternity in mind, they were thinking primarily of customers whose interest lay in local motorsport events. At the time when the first Bentley 3-litres left the Cricklewood works, there was also hope in the air that racing would resume at Brooklands.

Brooklands, near Weybridge in Surrey, was a legend in its own time. It was opened in June 1907 and was the first purpose-built banked motor racing circuit in the world. The man behind it was Hugh Locke-King, and a key factor in its birth was the restrictions placed on British motorists at the time. The Motor Car Act of 1903 limited speeds to 20mph on the road, and there were fears that this limitation would prevent motor manufacturers from carrying out sustained high-speed testing. So Brooklands, ostensibly at least, was built to allow British car makers to remain competitive with cars from other countries where there were no such speed restrictions.

The famous banked oval was surfaced in concrete because of the cost and difficulties of laying tarmac on the banking. The track was 100ft wide, and the circuit 2.75 miles long, with an additional "Finishing Straight" that bisected the oval and increased the track length by half a mile. Between 1907 and 1914, it became a hugely popular place to visit at weekends, and at its peak could accommodate 287,000 people. It offered an early 20th century alternative to a day at the horse races. Enthusiasts could enter the motor races (organised by various clubs); others could watch the races and enjoy a social day out; and from 1910 Brooklands was also the home of some of Britain's first flying schools.

The Bentley entry for the 1922 Indianapolis 500 race was chronologically the company's earliest "works" entry. It was not a great success. The specially-prepared 3-litre car is seen here during scrutineering for the event, where it was driven by Douglas Hawkes.

Later, the attractions of the circuit would be promoted with the slogan, "the right crowd and no crowding".

Brooklands' association with aviation saw it commandeered during the Great War of 1914-1918 as a centre for training Britain's military pilots. The track surface became damaged as the solid wheels of military trucks bit into the concrete. So it was a while before Brooklands opened for business again after the Armistice; but open it did, in 1921. In fact, the first major motor race held in England after the war was the Junior Car Club's 200-Mile Race at Brooklands in June that year. The circuit very quickly became a favourite weekend attraction again, and not surprisingly Bentley Motors seized on it as a place to demonstrate the excellence of the new 3-litre. If the car could be seen to do well in front of the Brooklands crowd, ran the thinking, it would very quickly attract interest and customers.

So Brooklands was a natural choice for the first appearance of a Bentley in motor sport. The event was the Essex Motor Club's race for cars with engines larger than 1700cc; the car was EXP2, the second experimental 3-litre; and the driver was Frank Clement. Clement, who would go on to run the Racing Shop at Cricklewood and become a valuable member of the "works" racing team, was the only professional driver on the Bentley staff at the time. He had been with Vauxhall, Napier and Star before joining Straker-Squire. There, he became a "works" driver by

1914 (and competed in the same 1914 TT race as WO did with the DFP) and, after war service in the Royal Engineers, he had gone back to Straker-Squire to become installation engineer and chief tester of the company's aero engines. He had met WO at the 1919 Olympia Show and joined Bentley Motors in 1920, taking Clive Gallop's place.

Contemporary accounts show that Clement and EXP 2 started well but that a misfire developed and that the car was running on only three of its four cylinders when the race ended. But it did finish. The race was won by Lionel Martin, driving an early example of the new Aston Martin. Martin's vision of the car he wanted to build was uncannily similar to WO's: he wanted his Aston Martin to be "a quality car of good performance and appearance; a car for the discerning owner driver with fast touring in mind – designed, developed, engineered and built as an individual."

Undeterred by this initial setback, Bentley Motors tried again, this time entering EXP2 at the Brooklands Whitsun meeting in June. In its first race, it was unplaced, but in its second race – a sprint event – it not only won but did so by "a comfortable margin" according to a report in *The Motor*. This was exactly the kind of publicity benefit that WO wanted. It got the Bentley marque talked about among the motor racing fraternity.

Brooklands would become an important showcase for the Bentley marque over the next decade – and indeed right through the 1930s, after the original company had been sold – as privateer drivers fought exciting duels in club racing events before large crowds. It would also become important to the Bentley factory as a place where chassis could be taken for high-speed testing. And it was a Brooklands regular, Bentley agent John Duff, who in 1922 would talk WO into entering cars for the new 24-hour event at Le Mans the following year.

1922 – Indianapolis and the TT

However, if exposure at Brooklands was a key element in WO's strategy for getting his new 3-litre known and talked about, it was certainly not the only one. Success at Brooklands was proof of high performance, but WO was also keen to demonstrate the reliability of his cars. This needed long-distance events, and he set his sights on two such events for the summer of 1922. One was the Indianapolis 500-Mile race that was to run on 30 May; the Indianapolis speedway was, of course, the American equivalent of Brooklands. The second was the Isle of Man Tourist Trophy event that would run very soon after it in June and would cover some 600 miles in two days. This would be the first TT to be held since 1914, and was bound to attract attention. As far as we can tell, the decision to run this limited "works" racing programme was taken in November 1921.

Entering two events so close to one another in time gave Bentley Motors a logistical problem. There was every chance that the car which ran at Indianapolis would not make it back across the Atlantic in time to run again on the Isle of Man, even if its crew did. So there would have to be four cars – more or less a full week's production of chassis at Cricklewood at the time – prepared as "works" racers. One would go to Indianapolis, and the other three would become the Bentley team for the TT.

Finding enough drivers also presented a few problems. Frank Clement was an obvious choice because he had already become the works competition driver, perhaps by default more than anything else. WO himself could fill a second seat, and his pre-war experience of the TT made him an obvious choice for that event. But there were no obvious third and fourth choices. So WO decided to employ a professional driver and Brooklands *habitué*, Douglas Hawkes, to tackle the Indianapolis event.

Douglas Hawkes made it back from the USA to drive a similar car in the Tourist Trophy event. The first of these pictures was taken during practice for the race; the second, taken during the race itself, shows how experience with the road conditions had persuaded the Bentley team to rig up a crude dust guard over the right-hand front wheel to protect the driver.

Assuming he got back in time, Hawkes would also take the third seat in the TT entry. Each driver needed a riding mechanic, who would have to be drawn from the ranks of Bentley mechanics familiar with the cars. So Clement was paired with Arthur Saunders (who had been FT Burgess's riding mechanic on the 1914 TT Humber), WO with Leslie Pennal, and Hawkes was allocated Bert Browning for both the Indianapolis and the TT entries.

The four chassis were handed over to Frank Clement in the Experimental Shop at Cricklewood in January 1922 for preparation. WO was

THE 1922 INDIANAPOLIS AND TT CARS

The Indianapolis car was:

Chassis no	Registration	Race no	Crew
94	ME 4976	22	Douglas Hawkes; riding mechanic Bert Browning

The three cars that ran in the 1922 TT race were as follows:

Chassis no	Registration	Race no	Crew
42	ME 1884	3	Frank Clement; riding mechanic Arthur Saunders
72	ME 3115	9	WO Bentley; riding mechanic Leslie Pennall
74	ME 3494	6	Douglas Hawkes; riding mechanic Bert Browning

The subsequent history of these four cars was complicated. The three TT cars appeared in a famous photograph wearing the wrong registration plates, which has confused many writers. Then all the TT cars had to be sold in order to raise money. The chassis of the Indianapolis car was given the body from the first TT car and was sold as that car. The first TT car was then re-numbered as the Indianapolis car and fitted with a special single-seater body. So the car now preserved in the Indianapolis Speedway Museum is probably not the actual car that Douglas Hawkes drove in the Indianapolis 500, but one of the TT team cars!

Surviving records show that the total cost of preparing all three TT team cars was just £75. However, mechanic Leslie Pennal remembered that there were "all sorts of special fittings" on them. "There was a terrific lot to do on everything," he told Elizabeth Nagle, and singled out the special midships-mounted petrol tanks with their large brass filler caps, special shock-absorber brackets, and a special oil tank.

clearly keen that they should be representative of the production 3-litre, and indeed he made the point forcefully just before the TT: "We would like to point out that, unlike our competitors, we have not built special racing cars for this event, but instead entered three standard chassis drawn from our production stock."

Standard chassis they may have been, but after Frank Clement had finished with them their resemblance to standard production chassis had become a little more distant. They had been fitted with long-range fuel tanks amidships, so that they could carry an extra 22 gallons of petrol and consequently go for longer between fuel stops. Their engines had been carefully prepared to give their best, with high-compression pistons and a racing carburettor, and there was a straight-through exhaust mounted alongside the body instead of under the chassis. The cars had special short, flat radiators which bore very little resemblance to the production type – in order to improve aerodynamics, according to some, although mechanic Wally Hassan told Elizabeth Nagle he thought they were a way of saving money. And all four cars had special lightweight aluminium two-seater bodies with no wings, built by Ewart's and fashioned along the lines of the body on WO's own 1914 Tourist Trophy DFP entry. The Indianapolis car had a longer tail than the other three.

The Indianapolis entry was not a great success. Although European cars had dominated the event between 1912 and 1914, by the early 1920s American builders were making determined efforts to win back their home event, and in fact the 1922 Indy 500 saw Jimmy Murphy romp home in first place with a Duesenberg chassis powered by a Harry Miller-designed 3-litre engine. Hawkes, Browning and the Bentley finished last in qualifying and last of the 13 finishers in the race; Hawkes was actually warned by the starter for driving a slow car in the centre of the track. "We were not fast enough," admitted WO in *An Illustrated History of the Bentley Car*, and entering for the Indy 500 "cost us rather a lot of money that we could not afford". But the fact was that the Bentley did finish, averaging 81.9mph over the 200 laps of the brick-paved speedway track; 14 other cars all failed to complete the race. However, most of the other cars were specially-prepared racing machines, so this was not as poor a result as it initially sounds because the Bentley was close to production standard. One modification made to the car was done to meet local requirements: the Americans insisted that it was fitted with a special steering wheel made from steel tubing because the hard surface of the raceway was notorious for breaking up standard types.

The TT was very different. Hawkes and Browning only just made it home in time, and the Indianapolis car – which would have been the spare team car had it been available – was still somewhere aboard a ship in the middle of the Atlantic. On the morning of the race, the heavens opened, and the Bentley team hurriedly strapped a plywood board to each car behind the right-hand front wheel to keep the spray from blinding the drivers.

WO did not enjoy the experience of driving in that race – the last one in which he would compete personally – but Bentley's efforts were rewarded by a complete lack of mechanical troubles (unless we count the broken exhaust and loose floorboards that afflicted WO's own car). The race went to Jean Chassagne in the "works" 3-litre Sunbeam racer, but Clement brought his Bentley home in second place, less than four minutes later. A Vauxhall 3-litre Grand Prix car came third, six seconds ahead of WO in fourth place. And right behind him in fifth place came Douglas Hawkes in the third Bentley, which had lost a plug and all of its water early in the race but had still survived until the end.

It was a tremendous result, not least because Vauxhall and Sunbeam had both fielded Grand Prix racers rather than production-type road cars. As the only complete three-car team to finish the race, Bentley Motors were awarded the Team Prize. Back home, the cars lined up for a now-famous photograph in which their identities were confused by swapped number-plates and further confused by having WO sitting in Hawkes's car and vice versa. It was to be Bentley's last TT, however. The 1922 race had been an odd one, allowing engine capacities up to 3 litres when the latest Grand Prix regulations were demanding engines no larger than 2 litres, and there followed a period of six years in which no more Tourist Trophy races were held. By the time the next one took place in 1928, the Bentley "works" team effort was almost single-mindedly focussed on Le Mans.

As for the Tourist Trophy race, the 1922 event was actually the only one to be held after the Great War at the Isle of Man Circuit. There was no Tourist Trophy race for cars between 1923 and 1927, and when the event returned to the racing calendar it had moved to the Ards circuit in Northern Ireland. None of this prevented Bentley Motors from capitalising on the event. As Chapter 2 explains, between late 1922 and 1924, they offered a special high-performance "TT" chassis as a standard production option.

Meanwhile, increasing numbers of 3-litre Bentleys were appearing in club events all over the country in the hands of privateers. Darrell Berthon estimated that Bentleys took no fewer than 19 first places in speed events between July and October 1922. Frank Clement found himself regularly appearing at hill-climb events with a car in support of the local Bentley agent, and in fact it was a local Bentley agent who took the marque on to its next major sporting achievements. The agent was John Duff, who in 1922 set up Duff and Aldington as a Bentley agency in London. Already a Brooklands regular, where he was known for racing big aero-engined cars, he decided to tackle the "Double Twelve" record at the circuit in a Bentley. The "Double Twelve" involved driving the car as far as possible in two 12-hour stints; a continuous 24-hour run was forbidden because local residents objected to the noise at night. The first event had been run earlier that year, when Captain Alastair Miller's overhead-camshaft Wolseley 10 Moth set the first record.

When word reached Bentley Motors about Duff's entry, WO seems to have been in no doubt that the company should lend it some unofficial support by providing a pair of mechanics for the weekend. John Duff had already carried out some tuning on the engine himself, but the Experimental Department at Cricklewood did some further preparation. They also lent Duff a team of mechanics to assist in preparing and running the car, and on 28 August 1922 he made his first attempt.

The car let him down before he could achieve his aim, but he had driven fast enough to set new Class E world records for 1, 2, and 3 hours,

---

THE 1922 DOUBLE TWELVE CAR

The details of the 1922 Double Twelve car were as follows:

Chassis no	Registration	Race no	Crew
141	XM 6761	5	John Duff

The birth of a legend: this is the start of the 1923 Le Mans 24-hour race, the first of its kind. John Duff's Bentley 3-litre was the only British car entered for the event, and is identifiable here from the number 8 painted on its radiator grille. Ahead of it are two 5.3-litre Excelsiors and a 3½-litre Lorraine-Dietrich.

100 and 200 miles, and 100, 200, 300, and 400 kilometres. Undaunted, he returned on September 27, and drove the 12-hour shift on that day and the 12-hour shift on the subsequent day single-handed. This time, he was successful, breaking the Double-Twelve record at an average speed of 86.52 mph and covering a total distance of 2082 miles. This run netted him a total of 38 international class records, including all the Class E world records for 1 to 12 hours and all distances from 100 to 1000 miles and 100 to 1600 kilometres.

Clearly, Duff was a man to be reckoned with, and the two mechanics allocated to support him, Leslie Pennal and Wally Hassan, were unanimous in their admiration for the toughness he displayed during the race. It would not be the last Bentley Motors would hear of John Duff, either. Later that year, he approached WO at

Bentley's offices in Hanover Square with a new idea. He had heard about a new 24-hour race to be run in France, on rural roads around the town of Le Mans, and he wanted Bentley Motors to provide "works" support when he entered a car.

1923 – the first Le Mans

WO was initially very much against the idea of entering this new 24-hour event in France. Though he recognised the potential value of such an event in proving Bentley reliability, he very much doubted whether any car – not even his own 3-litre – could survive racing for 24 hours continuously on the unmade roads so typical of France in those days. However, John Duff was not a man to be deterred, and eventually WO gave in.

There was a condition, though: even though Bentley Motors would lend Duff two mechanics as his pit crew and allow Frank Clement to act as his riding mechanic, this was most emphatically not going to be a Bentley "works" entry. The car would be entered by Duff and Aldington, John Duff's company. In the beginning, WO refused even to go and watch, but in the end curiosity got the better of him and he travelled to Le Mans with Bentley's Sales Manager, AFC Hillstead, arriving on the morning of 27 May 1923, the Saturday when the race was due to start.

THE 1923 LE MANS CAR

Details of John Duff's 1923 Le Mans car were as follows:

Chassis no	Registration	Race no	Crew
141	XM 6761	8	John Duff, Frank Clement

This car is the subject of a book written by Clare Hay and published in 2009: *Chassis 141: The Story of the First Le Mans Bentley.*

Duff's 3-litre Bentley was the only British entry in the field, and in fact the only car to start that was not French. The conditions were far from ideal. A hailstorm broke shortly after the race had begun, and that was followed by heavy rain that lasted for some four hours. At dusk, a stone went through one of the Bentley's headlights, but Duff continued to drive hard through the night – hard enough to set several lap records. Then another stone thrown up from the unmade roads went through the Bentley's petrol tank at about mid-day on the Sunday, and the subsequent fuel leak brought the car to a halt some three miles from the pits.

So Duff ran back all the way to the pits to get some cans of petrol. Frank Clement, awaiting his turn at the wheel, now took over. He "borrowed" a soldier's bicycle, slung the cans over his shoulder, and pedalled furiously back to the stranded car. With a chewing-gum patch on the hole in the tank and fuel replenished from the cans, he then nursed the Bentley back to the pits where the Bentley pit crew made a more lasting repair. He and Duff then shot off to record the fastest lap of the race (at 66.69mph) and to drive on as hard as they could. Despite losing some two and a half hours because of this punctured fuel tank, and despite a nasty

Conditions at the 1923 Le Mans event were basic, and this tent was the Bentley pit. John Duff is lying under his car, which was basically a Vanden Plas-bodied Speed Model with the narrow, flat wings favoured by sporting drivers at the time. There does not seem to be much sense of urgency in this picture!

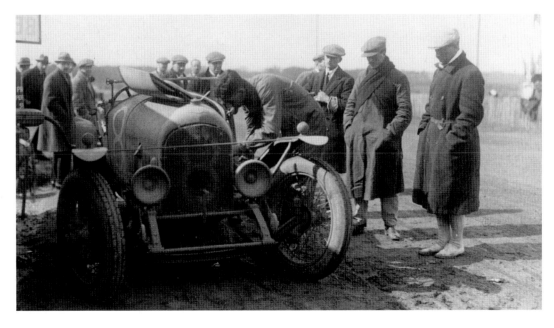

There is not much urgency here, either! Duff works on the engine of his 3-litre: stones have already taken care of the glass in the car's headlamps.

A Bentley at Brooklands: this is GF 330, here probably being driven by Frank Clement. The car was later rebodied for record attempts at *Monthléry but never seems to have had a chassis number: though that number was given as 400 at Montlhéry, chassis number 400 had probably not been built by the time this picture was taken in 1923!

moment when the Bentley's two-wheel brakes proved inadequate and Frank Clement had to take to an escape road at Mulsanne, they still managed to bring the car home in an exceptionally creditable fourth place.

It was a major achievement and, most importantly, it had persuaded WO himself of the value of the Le Mans race. Initially more than somewhat doubtful, the man behind Bentley Motors later admitted (in *An Illustrated History of the Bentley Car*): "After a few hours I began to enjoy life greatly, and to realise that this was a race that might have been instituted especially for our benefit."

Duff, however, was far from finished for 1923. Over the summer, he took his 3-litre to the Basque region of northern Spain for the Touring Grand Prix of Guipuzcoa, held near San Sebastian. His was one of two Bentley entries, the second being a locally-owned car which retired shortly before the end of the race. Duff took the lead on the fifth lap and held it for a further eight laps until a flying stone smashed his driving goggles and he lost control and crashed. But his average speed of 65mph up to that point was 10mph faster than the eventual race winner's average, and the race authorities were impressed enough to award him the prize money for the 3-litre class.

In September, he was back on the Continent with his car, this time for the Georges Boillot Cup held on 23 miles of rural roads around Boulogne in France. On this occasion, his was one of a team of three Bentleys, the other two being "works" cars driven by Frank Clement and Service Manager Bertie Kensington-Moir. The results were not so good: Kensington-Moir was the only driver to finish, and that well down the field. In a classic case of racing being used to improve the breed, his car had an experimental carburettor installation of twin Zenith RA48s fitted with heating coils, and these gave trouble during the race. Clement's car had been fitted with experimental magnesium alloy pistons, and these too gave trouble so that he was out of the race by the second lap. Duff was eventually forced to retire when his car caught fire as a result of damage sustained when he had hit a cow during the practice laps.

THE 1923 SPANISH GP CAR

Chassis no	Registration	Race no	Crew
141	XM 6761	10	John Duff

THE 1923 BOILLOT CUP CARS

Chassis no	Registration	Race no	Crew
7*	XH 9047	26	Bertie Kensington-Moir
141	XM 6761	21	John Duff
246	MF 1900	25	Frank Clement

*Rebuilt in 1926 and re-numbered NR520, registration MK 2941

The photograph has been heavily retouched, but this is unmistakeably the 1924 Le Mans Bentley, driven by John Duff with Frank Clement. Note the size of the crowd: the new event had quickly caught the public's imagination.

1924 – the first Le Mans win

Bentley were back at Le Mans in mid-June 1924 and, as in 1923, they were the only non-French starters. Once again, there was just one car, and once again the crew was Duff and Clement. This time, however, the name of the entrant was given as Bentley Motors. The car was a new one, with a production-style four-seat touring body. It also boasted the front-wheel brakes which were just about to enter production for the 1924-season 3-litres, and it had been prepared with stoneguards to protect the head-lamps and grille. Duff had also lagged the fuel tank to prevent a recurrence of the problems in the 1923 event.

This year, the race organisers had introduced a new and, to modern eyes, somewhat bizarre requirement. Open cars had to stop after five laps to raise their hoods, and then had to run for at least 20 laps with the hood up. After that, the hood had to be checked by race officials. There was potential for losing a lot of valuable time in this, and so John Duff prepared for the race by practising raising and lowering the hood of his car without getting out of the driver's seat. By race time, he had got his time down to 40 seconds.

It all helped, but the key factors in the Bentley's race were its speed and reliability. As other cars dropped out of the race one by one, the Bentley kept going. WO had arranged for pit signals to be relayed by telephone to members of the pit crew stationed at Mulsanne, and this allowed valuable information to be communicated to the driver more than once on every lap. Yet the Bentley's race was not without incident. First of all, the gear-change jammed when a coachbuilder's staple somehow found its way into the gate. Then the windscreen broke off, and swollen hubs delayed the car for some 40 minutes while a wheel was changed. But Duff and Clement brought their car home in first place. "We won by some 90 miles over the Lorraines," wrote WO in *An Illustrated History of the Bentley Car*, "even though only 10 of these miles were shown in the record due to a misunderstanding". He went on to add, "The 1924 Le Mans was a most important race for us. Not only did it help our sales, and help me in my almost non-stop contest with the Board over racing; it filled us all with a spirit of new self-confidence. In fact it made us rather too pleased with ourselves, and it would have been better for our souls if we had not been so successful so early!"

Perhaps most revealing in that comment is the reference to WO's "contest with the Board".

John Duff entered Le Mans again in 1924, and the stoneguards over the headlights on his car reflect lessons learned in 1923. He now has four-wheel brakes. Here he is lowering the hood on his car: the 1924 regulations required cars to run for 20 laps with hoods up.

THE 1924 LE MANS CAR

Details of John Duff's 1924 Le Mans car were as follows:

Chassis no	Registration	Race no	Crew
582	XT 1606	8	John Duff and Frank Clement

had too little of it. It was always difficult to persuade those who had sunk their money into Bentley Motors and become Directors of the company that racing success would eventually pay dividends. But those most closely involved with the "works" team understood what WO was trying to achieve, and understood the potential publicity benefits. The 1924 Le Mans race was run in dry conditions, and the winning Bentley finished the race relatively unscathed. John Duff thought that the British public would not appreciate the magnitude of the Bentley achievement if they saw photographs of a clean car and so, before the official post-race pictures were taken, he brushed some mud onto it to make it look the part.

1925 – a failure at Le Mans

The Bentley works team effort once again focussed exclusively on Le Mans for 1925. This time, things were just a little more serious, and two cars rather than one were entered. John Duff entered his own car, technically as a privateer but with support from Cricklewood, and the second car was an official "works" entry.

Bentley Motors were not alone in seeing Le Mans as an event that really mattered, and this

The Bentley pits at Le Mans in 1925. John Duff again entered, and his car is on the left. The other car was prepared for Bertie Kensington-Moir and Dudley Benjafield. Neither covered itself in glory. Miscalculations about fuel consumption put both cars out of the race, and WO described this setback as a "disaster".

year they were not the only non-French entrants. Of the 68 entries (a number whittled down to 49 starters), there were seven from Italy, six from Great Britain, and two from the USA.

Duff once again had his regular co-driver, Frank Clement. The "works" Bentley was in the hands of Dr Dudley Benjafield, a gifted amateur driver, and Bertie Kensington-Moir. Both were new cars, and both had open four-seater bodies. The Benjafield car was Bentley's first proper "works" car, if the 1922 TT cars are discounted, and it was essentially a standard Speed model with the latest twin SU "sloper" carburettors and a Vanden Plas open four-seater body. Carefully prepared, like the Duff car, by Frank Clement in the Experimental Shop, it had been fitted with a 25-gallon fuel tank in place of the standard 16-gallon item and with mesh stoneguards over the radiator and headlights.

This year, there were some more new regulations, to make things more interesting. One introduced the famous "Le Mans start", where drivers have to sprint across the pit lane to board their vehicles; another forbade refuelling before the 20th lap.

Unfortunately, pre-race calculations had not

Unfortunately, pre-race calculations had not allowed for the effect on fuel consumption of the "raised hoods" regulation, which still applied. Early on in the race, Bertie Kensington-Moir at the wheel of the number two car became embroiled in a duel with the vastly experienced Sir Henry Segrave, driving a Sunbeam. Over some 15 laps, his enthusiasm caused him to use more fuel than he had planned, with the result that he ran out of petrol before the 20th lap and was forced to retire.

The number one car fared little better, although it lasted longer. In what must have seemed like an agonising *déjà vu* incident, the Duff-Clement car ran out of fuel before completing its 20th lap. Duff ran back to the pits to get some, ignored WO's comment that this was breaking the rules, and set off again. This breach of regulations was nevertheless prevented from becoming a major incident when a carburettor float chamber broke off early in the morning of the second day's racing. The car caught fire and was too badly damaged to repair. So Duff and Clement were forced to retire.

"The disaster of 1925 was a great blow to us," wrote WO in *An Illustrated History of the Bentley Car*. "We could not afford this sort of setback, and the Board was the first to recognise it. I came in for a good deal of criticism, and quite rightly. All I could do was recommend strongly that we should return in strength the following year, and assure them that there would be no mistakes this time."

But John Duff, at least, had every intention of making up for the Le Mans disappointment. That September, and with the support of Bentley Motors, he was at the Montlhéry circuit, France's answer to Brooklands, with a determined plan to secure more records with his Bentley. The car now looked very different from its Le Mans days, having been re-bodied by Weymann as a single-seater. This time, Duff's aim was the Class D 24-hour world speed record, and as his co-driver he took with him Dudley Benjafield. Their first attempt was unsuccessful, but at their second attempt on 21-22 September they did it. The 3-litre Bentley came away with the new record of 95.03mph over 2280.69 miles. It was a stunning achievement, but it did not bring joy to the Boardroom at Bentley Motors, for by this time things were looking very gloomy indeed on the financial front.

John Duff's 1925 Le Mans car was, strictly, a private entry. Car number 10 was prepared specially for the event and thus became Bentley Motors' first "works" team car since the 1922 Indianapolis and TT events. Note the huge klaxon horn on the running-board: Le Mans was still run over public roads in those days.

THE 1925 LE MANS CARS

Details of the 1925 Le Mans cars were as follows:

Chassis no	Registration	Race no	Crew
1040	MD 7187	9	John Duff and Frank Clement
1138	MH 7580	10	Bertie Kensington-Moir and Dudley Benjafield

Note: Although chassis number 1040 wore registration number MD 7187 for the Le Mans event, its correct registration was in fact YM 7646

THE 1925 MONTLHÉRY CAR

Details of the 1925 Montlhéry car were as follows:

Chassis no	Registration	Race no	Crew
1040	YM 7646	N/A	John Duff and Woolf Barnato

This was John Duff's 1925 Le Mans car, rebuilt, rebodied and wearing its correct registration number.

1926 – Montlhéry and Le Mans

By the time the international racing season got under way in 1926, Bentley Motors had changed hands. The deal with Woolf Barnato had been done in March, and there would in future be more careful control of expenditure in all areas, including motorsport. However, the Bentley team had already made its plans for the season, and so they went ahead. The two key events were both in June; one was Le Mans, but this would be preceded by an attempt on more records at Montlhéry. Inspired no doubt by John Duff's efforts the previous September, Bentley Motors decided to see if they could improve on his record with a "works" car.

The car was specially built for the job,

THE 1926 MONTLHÉRY CAR

Details of the 1926 *Montlhéry car were as follows:

Chassis no	Registration	Race no	Crew
"400"	MF330	N/A	Woolf Barnato, Dudley Benjafield, Frank Clement and George Duller

Known as the Slug because of its appearance, this car also ran with a long streamlined tail by Gordon England. Its chassis number was recorded as 400, although chassis 400 actually belonged to another car altogether. The Slug was more commonly known as the "No2 two-seater".

THE 1926 LE MANS CARS

Details of the 1926 Le Mans cars were as follows:

Chassis no	Registration	Race no	Crew
LM1344	MK 5206	7	Dudley Benjafield and Sammy Davis
LM1345	MK 5205	8	Frank Clement and George Duller
1179	KM 4250	9	Scrap Thistlethwayte and Clive Gallop

THE 1926 BOILLOT CUP CAR

Details of the 1926 Boillot Cup car were as follows:

Chassis no	Registration	Race no	Crew
LM1344	MK 5206	45	Dudley Benjafield and Bertie Kensington-Moir

---

although money was tight (as usual) and in fact the basis of the record-breaker was Dudley Benjafield's own short-chassis Brooklands racer. This was fitted with a special lightweight body. Four drivers were selected: Benjafield himself, Frank Clement, Woolf Barnato (who already had a formidable reputation at Brooklands and elsewhere) and another "new boy", George Duller. Duller was a former champion jockey who had turned to motorsport and had competed at both Brooklands and Le Mans.

The first attempt was made on 1 June. All was going well until Duller spun the car, came into the pits and found that all the other drivers were away resting. Wally Hassan, who was a mechanic on the pit crew, stepped into the breach, raced off in the car and crashed after only a third of a lap, nearly killing himself. The team had achieved the 12-hour record with an average speed of 97.54mph, but could go no further on that occasion.

On the second attempt, a few days later, the car went well but was again unable to complete the full 24-hour stretch. The Bentley team had to be content with the Six Hour record at 102.2mph. For the third attempt, the car was fitted with a streamlined body with a long tail (following the little-understood principles of improving aerodyanamics). Again the attempt started well, and the car beat its own 12-hour record with an average speed of 100.96mph. But some four hours later it crashed during a thunderstorm, and that was the end of the Bentley attempt. The team had other things to do. Le Mans was just a few days away.

This was the year's first disappointment. The second was that the 1926 Bentley assault on Le Mans did not turn out quite as well as WO had promised the Bentley Motors Board it would. Despite excellent performances during the race, one by one the three 3-litre Bentleys were eliminated – the last one when within striking distance of a place in the top three finishers. "Lack of preparation, due to our preoccupation with record-breaking at Montlhéry, was certainly a contributory cause," was WO's rather rueful comment many years later in *An Illustrated History of the Bentley Car*.

This time, Bentley Motors entered two cars and supported a third private entry. The company's own cars were both Speed models, and the third car was a Supersports; to meet Le Mans regulations, coachbuilder Martin Walter

Le Mans in 1926 was another disaster for the Bentley team, and WO felt the humiliation keenly. The 3-litres were over-stretched as they tried to keep up with the 3½-litre Lorraine-Dietrich cars and, one by one, all three Bentleys were forced to retire. This was the start of the race, with the Benjafield-Davis 3-litre wearing race number 7.

managed to squeeze four seats into the ultra-short 9ft wheelbase of the 100mph car.

In previous years, the crews had been clearly composed of one driver and one riding mechanic, even if the riding mechanic himself was no mean driver as well. For 1926, the focus was on the drivers. The first Speed model was given to Dudley Benjafield and Sammy Davis, motorsport correspondent of *The Autocar* and a long-term friend of WO's. The second Speed model was allocated to Frank Clement and George Duller. The privately-owned Supersports car was driven by its owner Tom "Scrap" Thistlethwayte, and Clive Gallop, who had been among those involved with the design and construction of the 3-litre engine at the turn of the decade.

The race began well for the Bentleys, and by 4am on the Sunday morning the three cars were lying in 5th, 7th and 8th places. But then things began to go wrong, for the pace set by the 3½-litre Lorraine-Dietrich cars was proving too much. The first Bentley to retire was the Duller car, suffering from valve stretch caused by over-revving, 72 laps in, at about six o'clock in the morning. Three hours later, Clive Gallop was forced to stop with a broker rocker arm. The Davis-Benjafield car had by then fought its way up to third place, and stood a good chance of staying there. But in a burst of enthusiasm to improve their position about 20 minutes before the end of the race, Sammy Davis overdid things

at Mulsanne and rammed the car into a sand-bank from which it proved impossible to extract it. Bentley was out, and Lorraine-Dietrich went on to an impressive 1-2-3 victory.

"Nothing worse, we felt afterwards, could now happen to us. It was a disaster." With those few words WO summed up the way the whole team must have felt. "Nothing can be worse for a team than to suffer defeats at an accelerating rate like this after reaching the heights: our humiliation was complete, and I was almost forced into the position of terminating our

George Duller, seated at the wheel of car no 15 in this shot, was a new boy in the Bentley team for 1926. A former champion jockey, he had gained a reputation as a racing driver as well. Segrave is sitting on the tail of no 14.

The idea of racing against the wind resistance from a billowing hood seems bizarre today, but it was part of the regulations in 1925. Cars would obviously have suffered from the same problem in high-speed driving on ordinary roads. This is the Benjafield-Davis car at speed.

made; he wanted to see some return on his investment in Bentley Motors. If Bentley were to continue racing – and there was every reason to agree with WO that racing success delivered the publicity that the marque needed – things were going to have to be better organised. For a start, the "team" cars could no longer be modified production cars. Instead, there would be a separate Racing Shop which would build proper "works" racers, even though these would be based on the production cars and would resemble them closely.

1927 – Success and glory

There was evidence of the new approach as the 1927 season opened. In May, the Bentley "works" team used the Essex Motor Club's Six Hour race at Brooklands as a dry run for Le Mans. The primary organisers were Dudley Benjafield and Sammy Davis, both keen to salvage their reputations after the humiliating near-miss at Le Mans the previous year. Davis, however, entered the race in an Alvis, allowing his seat in one of the "works" cars to be used for trying out another new driver. George Duller was there, too, but in a 3-litre Sunbeam.

modest racing programme."

Things did not improve later in the season, either. Dudley Benjafield decided to buy the car in which he had partnered Sammy Davis at Le Mans, and in September he took it to Boulogne for the Georges Boillot Cup race. Bertie Kensington-Moir had been one of the Bentley team drivers at this event in 1923, and this year he partnered Benjafield in the car. The pair were holding third place on the 13th lap when they crashed out of the race.

The 1926-season setbacks caused a re-think at Cricklewood, and no doubt Woolf Barnato was closely involved in the new plans that were

Driving "Old No 7", the car that Sammy Davis had ingloriously rammed into a sandbank at Le Mans, were Dudley Benjafield and Woolf Barnato. Leslie Callingham, who was associated with the oil company Shell, took the wheel of

Sammy Davis looks a little apprehensive as he sits at the wheel of one of the 1927 team cars at the pre-race scrutineering.

Come Le Mans 1927, Bentley Motors were taking no chances of further humiliation. They entered a three-car team. These are the drivers, seen before the event. From the left, Frank Clement and Leslie Callingham, André d'Erlanger and George Duller, and Sammy Davis and Dudley Benjafield. Behind d'Erlanger is Woolf Barnato, who was by this time Bentley's Chairman, while WO stands smiling behind and between Duller and Davis.

the second car, and Frank Clement drove the third. There was a fourth Bentley in the race, too, this one privately owned by Sir Henry "Tim" Birkin, and co-driven by Birkin and his brother Archie.

As far as the Bentley team were concerned, the main point of the event was to try out such things as pit drills, and they also used it to test out the latest innovation of lightweight duralumin rockers on the 3-litre engines. The pit drills went fine but the rockers began to break up during the race. Results were perhaps the least important outcome, and serial rocker failures ensured that none of the three 'team' cars finished.

However, this event did draw Bentley Motors' attention to Tim Birkin's abilities. They had already had an eye on him, and had offered him the chance to run the new duralumin rockers in his car, but Birkin, instinctively distrusting something new and unproven, declined. When Archie Birkin's driving in the early stages of the race proved somewhat wild and erratic, and Frank Clement's car was eliminated with rocker problems, the decision was taken to have Clement replace Archie in the Birkin car. Despite a broken gearbox which left them with only third gear, Tim Birkin and Frank Clement managed to finish the race third on distance and 8th on handicap. A year later, Birkin would find

THE 1927 SIX HOURS CARS

Details of the 1927 Six Hours cars were as follows:

Chassis no	Registration	Race no	Crew
RT1541	YO 3595	6	Leslie Callingham and Cyril Harvey
LM1344	MK 5206	10	Woolf Barnato and Dudley Benjafield
BL1601	YE 6029	11	Tim Birkin and Archie Birkin; Frank Clement replaced Archie Birkin during the race
LM1345	MK 5205	12	Frank Clement (retired but replaced Archie Birkin in car no 11)

THE 1927 LE MANS CARS

Details of the 1927 Le Mans cars were as follows:

Chassis no	Registration	Race no	Crew
ST3001 (4?-litre)	YH 3196	1	Leslie Callingham and Frank Clement
ML1501	YF 2503	2	André D'Erlanger and George Duller
LM1344	MK 5206	3	Dudley Benjafield and Sammy Davis

Le Mans 1927, and they're off! The three Bentleys are in the foreground of this picture, with the new 4½-litre in front, the Benjafield-Davis car under way, and the d'Erlanger-Duller pairing a little slower to start in car number 2.

himself driving for Bentley Motors.

As it happened, circumstances had already made the Bentley team favourites for the 1927 Le Mans event. Mergers, bankruptcies and other business problems had reduced the number of other manufacturers who fielded teams, and although earlier events had attracted nearly 50 entries, there were just 23 for 1927. Notable by their absence were the Lorraine-Dietrich team, who had won in 1925 and 1926.

Even so, there was more evidence of the Bentley team's determination to do the job properly as Le Mans approached. A week before the actual event, which began on 18 June, the whole team was already at Le Mans to practice. This time, the team again consisted of three cars, and one of them was the prototype 4½-litre, familiarly known as "Old Mother Gun". The other two were 3-litres, and one of them was Dudley Benjafield's car, "Old No 7". The cars ran for the first time with a brake modification in which the Perrot shafts were set up with their operating levers going up rather than down; the effect of this was that as the axle wound up on the springs, so it pushed the brakes on harder.

WO's plan was for the new 4½-litre to be driven by Frank Clement and Sammy Davis, but Davis wanted to stay partnered with Dudley Benjafield, no doubt to avenge their failure at the 1926 event. So the eventual line-up was Clement and Leslie Callingham in the 4½-litre, Benjafield and Davis in "Old No 7", and George

---

THE 1927 BOILLOT CUP CAR

Details of the 1927 Boillot Cup car were as follows:

Chassis no	Registration	Race no	Crew
LM1345	MK 5205	26	Leslie Callingham (replaced Scott as original entrant)

THE 1927 PARIS GP CARS

Details of the 1927 Paris GP car were as follows:

Chassis no	Registration	Race no	Crew
ST3001 (4½-litre)	YH 3196	2	Frank Clement and George Duller

Rudimentary protection for the public was still considered enough, and this splendidly atmospheric picture shows how the race must have looked to spectators. Just rounding the bend is the d'Erlanger-Duller 3-litre, still with its hood erect as required in the early stages of the race, followed by a 2-litre Th. Schneider.

Duller with Baron André d'Erlanger in the second 3-litre. D'Erlanger was a financier and playboy whom Barnato had recruited to the team. Barnato himself did not drive, pleading a prior business commitment on the Saturday, and his decision not to participate has been the subject of a great deal of speculation ever since. Benjafield's car was officially lent to Bentley Motors for the race so that it would be under the total control of WO as team manager.

The event rules this year demanded that the cars ran with their hoods erected for the first three hours of the race, and the drivers had to erect the hoods from their stowed position after sprinting across the track at the start. As expected, the 4½-litre, running as No 1, got away in first place. Benjafield and Davis in car no 3 settled into second place, while d'Erlanger and Duller in car no 2 maintained station in third place. The 4½-litre, at this stage being driven by Clement, was very fast indeed and not only broke the circuit record on its second lap but continued to improve on this time over the laps that followed, reaching a best average speed of 73.40mph.

The Bentleys did not have things all their own way, even in the early stages of the race, but by the Saturday evening they had lapped several of the slower cars. It was one of these cars, a Schneider 25SP driven by Poitier and Tabourin,

Leslie Callingham (left) and Frank Clement (right) drove the prototype 4½-litre but were involved in the White House crash.

that finished up broadside across the road after its driver entered the Maison Blanche (White House) corner too fast. Callingham, right behind him in the 4½-litre Bentley, avoided ramming the Schneider by heading for a ditch, but the car rolled and threw him into the middle of the road. The second Schneider then came round the corner at speed and was unable to avoid the stationary cars, colliding with both. Callingham meanwhile had started to walk back towards Arnage to warn the oncoming cars, but he was not in time to warn Duller in the 3-litre Bentley, who rounded the corner and hit the wreckage, pushing the 4½-litre back onto the road.

Straight after that, a 2-litre Aries ploughed into the wreckage. There was by now so much

The infamous White House crash occurred after dark, and no photographs were taken. This drawing by Brian de Grineau nevertheless gives a good impression of the scene.

A pit stop for the Benjafield-Davis car, now bent and battered after its White House encounter.

debris scattered across the road that some was visible from the far side of the corner, and Sammy Davis spotted it as he approached White House. Instinctively recognizing that something was wrong, although not yet sure what it might be, he slowed for the corner but came upon the tangled mass of cars too late to stop. So he slewed the Bentley around to crash into the wreckage of Duller's Bentley broadside on at about 80mph, severely damaging the right-hand front side of his own car.

Unlike the others, he was able to re-start and so, after checking that there were no major casualties at the scene, he drove cautiously on to the pits. The rules insisted that only drivers could work on the cars, so he and Dudley Benjafield re-attached the right-hand front wing with string and replaced the terminally broken headlamp with a torch attached to the windscreen frame. Front axle, right-hand front wheel and chassis were all bent, but Davis insisted on carrying on and checked the car's behaviour over six laps before changing places with Benjafield.

The Bentley had now slipped a long way down the field, but Dudley Benjafield pushed the car as hard as he dared to regain the lead, profiting from mechanical problems that forced the leading Aries of Chassagne and Laly into the pits. At the end of one lap, Benjafield pulled into the pits and insisted that Sammy Davis should drive the car to the finish. Though running at reduced speeds, Davis managed to pass the leading car during the final hour of the race and nursed the Bentley home to gain first place with an average speed of 61.354mph. They had covered just 1472.527 miles in the 24 hours, a total far below the previous year's record of 1586 miles and one indicative of the problems that resulted from the White House crash.

The real significance of the Bentley victory at Le Mans in 1927 went beyond the obvious. Nicholas Foulkes neatly summed it up in his book *The Bentley Era*: "It is safe to say that Bentley's Le Mans success captured the imagination of the nation. Had the race been as uneventful as it initially seemed, and had Bentleys taken the flag in first, second and third place, as looked possible, would the 1927 victory have had such an impact? Probably not. It was the drama of the circumstances, the pluck of the drivers, and the fact that a British team had come back from near-certain defeat to see off competition from all over the world that shaped the Bentley image."

After the triumph of Le Mans, anything else was bound to be something of an anti-climax. Not that this prevented some of the Bentley Boys from at least trying. For the Boillot Cup handicap race at Boulogne in September, the spare Le Mans car (a third car prepared for the event but not actually used) was entered in the name of WB Scott, a recent addition to the

The pressure is on, and the only surviving Bentley – also the only large car left in the race – desperately tries to make up time on the Sunday afternoon.

Bentley coterie. In fact, it was Leslie Callingham who drove in the race, but he retired with mechanical problems. Then the Le Mans 4½-litre car, rebuilt after its crash at White House Corner, went to Montlhéry for the Paris Grand Prix. Here, it performed well in the hands of Clement and Duller, coming home in first place a full nine laps ahead of the second-placed 1100cc BNC of Doré and Pousse.

Celebrating in style: this was the menu – signed by the members of the victorious Bentley team – from the celebration dinner held at the Savoy Hotel in London in June 1927.

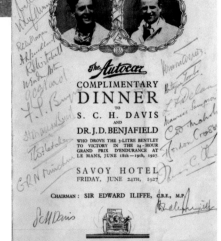

Done it! Cars line up after the event. Davis and Benjafield are on the winning Bentley, with the second-placed 1100cc Salmson and the seventh-placed front-wheel-drive Tracta alongside.

145

Racing green?

The colour green is so inextricably associated with the racing Bentleys that it is worth explaining its origins. In the 1900 Gordon Bennett Cup, established for motor racing teams representing different nations, the participating nations chose different colours to make their cars more readily recognisable. France chose blue, Belgium yellow, Germany white and America red. When Britain entered the 1901 event, SF Edge had his 50hp Napier painted green. So green became the British international racing colour. Nowadays, it is invariably called British Racing Green (which is more a legend than a precise colour). The original colour was always called Napier Green.

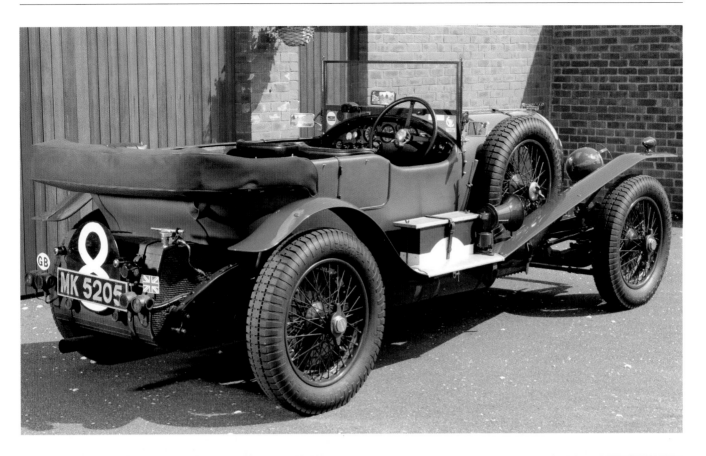

Although the shade of green arouses regular comment, paint of this shade was found on the car when it was restored. LM1345, driven by Frank Clement and George Duller in the 1926 Le Mans, is now owned by James Medcalf. Note the klaxon on the running-board - necessary because the Le Mans event was run on public roads.

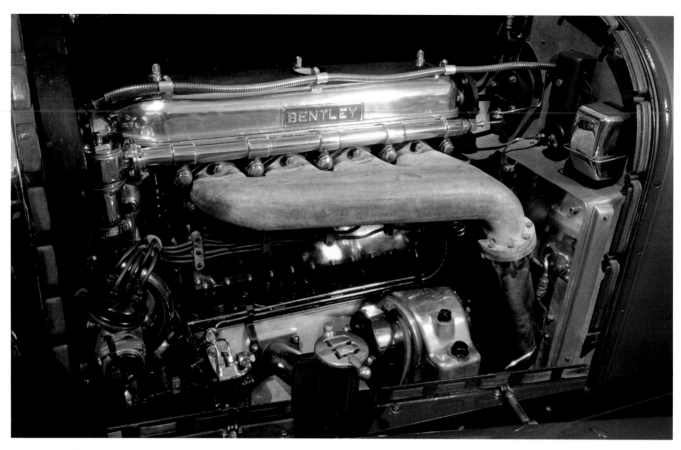

The Le Mans car's engine is externally
hard to distinguish from a standard
production Speed Model engine of the
time; the extended oil filler is the only
obvious clue here. The secret lay in
meticulous engine preparation at
Cricklewood to ensure that an engine
gave of its best.

Confirmation that this is the original
engine, number LM 1342 – and
further confirmation of its
competition career in the RAC
scrutineers' marks.

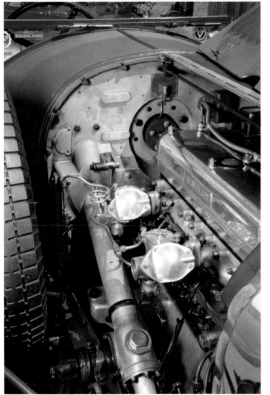

The Le Mans car used the most powerful version of the 3-litre engine available at the time, with twin SU G5 "sloper" carburettors. Note the split-pinned securing nut.

The array of instruments was essentially the same as on a standard production model, with a speedometer that read to just 100mph.

Despite the short wheelbase, LM 1345 was a full four-seater car. Bodywork was by Vanden Plas.

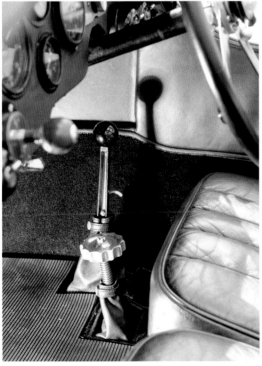

The cockpit of LM 1345 does not immediately suggest that it was a team car. Note, however, the spring-spoke steering wheel and the large screw control which made brake adjustment quicker and easier than on the standard cars. The team cars had folding windscreens at this stage, as they had to complete a number of laps at Le Mans with the hood erect.

Stoneguards on the headlights reduced the risk of problems during the night-time racing at Le Mans.

A quick-release filler cap was used on the radiator.

The fuel tank was larger than standard, and was protected against stone damage by wooden slatting and the same type of wire mesh used to cover the lights. The special Le Mans fuel filler makes an interesting comparison with the quick-release type that features on the Birkin supercharged car illustrated in Chapter 6.

Bentley never did take chances with the wheel securing nuts: there are clear instructions stamped into the outer section.

Not seen on the standard production models was this shielding, fitted to protect the underside from stone damage.

Experience had shown the need for rapid accessibility when something went wrong, and the team cars had an extended oil filler; to top up the oil, the bonnet did not have to be opened.

The Le Mans specification included twin friction dampers on the rear axle. Note also how the springs have been bound for additional durability.

The chassis number on the frame is often hard to find under layers of paint - but somebody made a special effort to uncover it in order to prove the identity of this very special car.

Chapter Nine

Motorsport
The 4½-Litre Era

The 1927 season would be the last one for the 3-litre Bentleys in the "works" team. For 1928, the new and much faster 4½-litres would take over. In tandem with the extra care that was being given to car preparation in the Racing Shop at Cricklewood, a greater degree of professionalism was gripping the Bentley racing team. But something else was happening, too: the drivers were beginning to

change. Though there was no doubt that the dedicated, talented drivers of the earlier days had known how to enjoy themselves at pre-event and post-event parties, their numbers were increasingly becoming leavened by wealthy socialites who brought both talent and a different lifestyle to the team.

That they had skill, determination and courage behind the wheel of a Bentley was

Put out of action by the White House crash at the 1927 Le Mans, the first 4½-litre car, ST3001, returned to the Bentley team for the 1928 event. Here it is landing at Dieppe, on the way to the event.

undoubted, and it would be unfair to present them as caricatures in any way. But there was no doubt that Woolf Barnato himself, and the other drivers he attracted to the Bentley team, were rather larger than life, and did know how to party hard. These were the Bentley Boys and, as Nicholas Foulkes has put it, "while WO built the cars, the Bentley Boys built the brand". Their carefree and spendthrift lifestyle kept them in the headlines as celebrities in their own right. They were the 1920s counterparts of film stars, rock stars and Premier League footballers in more recent years, their exploits being perfectly in keeping with what was expected of their kind in the Roaring Twenties.

1928 – the 4½-litre team

The team focussed on Le Mans for 1928, held this year on 16 and 17 June, but used the Brooklands Six Hours event on 12 May as a dry run once again. The three "works" 4½-litres consisted of the 1927 prototype car (by now known as Old Mother Gun) and were to have included the two new 1928 team cars, but only one of these was ready in time. So Bernard Rubin (a close friend of Barnato's) lent his own 4½-litre to the factory as a substitute for the second car. There were also two private entries in 3-litres. Tim Birkin finished third with the new team car, Dudley Benjafield and Bernard Rubin came sixth, and Woolf Barnato with Frank Clement came eighth after some brake trouble. The three team Bentleys claimed the Team Prize for the event, and Barnato set the fastest lap.

It is to Barnato's great credit that he happily submitted to team discipline even though he was Chairman of the company. For Le Mans, he was allocated to drive Old Mother Gun in

The traditional Le Mans start, this time in 1928. A pair of Bentleys are visible in the middle distance, led by car number 3, which was driven by Tim Birkin and Jean Chassagne. Car number 1, Brisson's 4.9-litre Stutz, finished second.

Car number 4, assigned to Woolf Barnato and Bernard Rubin, passing Samuelson's Lagonda, which is stuck in a sandbank at Mulsanne, during the 1928 Le Mans.

The Benjafield-Clement car tackles Pontlieue corner on the Le Mans circuit, pursued by Brisson's Stutz.

THE 1928 SIX HOURS CARS

Details of the 1928 Six Hours cars were as follows:

Chassis no	Registration	Race no	Crew
ST3001	YH 3196	4	Frank Clement and Woolf Barnato
KM3077	YV 7263	5	Tim Birkin
HF3187	YU 3250	6	Bernard Rubin and Dudley Benjafield
ML1513 3-litre	YV 8585	7	Humphrey Cook
ML1501 3-litre	YE 6029	8	WB "Bummer" Scott

THE 1928 LE MANS CARS

Details of the 1928 Le Mans cars were as follows:

Chassis no	Registration	Race no	Crew
KM3088	YW 2557	2	Dudley Benjafield and Frank Clement
KM3077	YV 7263	3	Tim Birkin and Jean Chassagne
ST3001	YH 3196	4	Woolf Barnato and Bernard Rubin

tandem with Bernard Rubin. The second and third cars were the new 4½-litres; one was allocated to Dudley Benjafield and Frank Clement, and the other to Tim Birkin, who was paired with the legendary French driver Jean Chassagne. Both new cars had a new variant of the Vanden Plas open four-seater body, often referred to as the "bobtail". It had a tail that was partially faired in to enclose a vertical spare wheel and the D-shaped 25-gallon fuel tank, together with cycle-type front and rear wings. All the 1928 Le Mans team cars carried a third headlamp, fitted on a cross-bar between the main lamps and intended to improve the driver's ability to see the road during the night sections of the race.

Least fortunate was the Benjafield-Clement car, which suffered a cracked chassis that in turn provoked a water leak from the engine and was forced to retire. Birkin and Chassagne drove strongly, but when a tyre blew at speed Birkin carried on and buckled the wheel. Repairing the damage cost a three-hour delay, but the Birkin car still managed to finish in fifth place and to break the lap record at 79.33mph. Barnato and Rubin drove a superb and determined race, and their car also cracked its chassis close to the end. This caused the radiator hose to come off

The Benjafield-Clement car leads the Barnato-Rubin entry on a typical section of the Le Mans course. The third headlamp was intended to improve vision at night, but during the day was wrapped like the other lights as a protective measure.

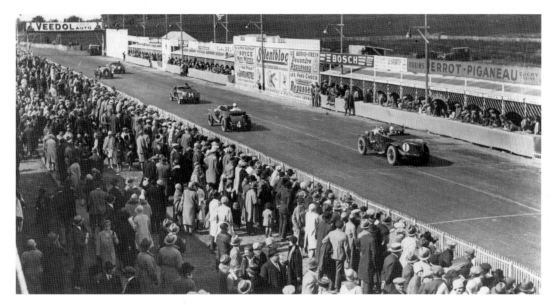

The view across the track past the pits at Le Mans, 1928. Car number 4, Old Mother Gun, driven by Barnato and Rubin, would go on to win.

its mounting and resulted in another water leak, but Barnato managed to nurse the car to the finish and to victory, just one lap ahead of the second-placed 4.9-litre Stutz Blackhawk driven by Brisson and Bloch. The Barnato-Rubin car had covered 1658.654 miles in the 24 hours, at an average speed of 69.11mph.

The indefatigable Tim Birkin was determined to push Bentley successes even further, and over the summer of that year he entered three other major events to fly the flag for Bentley. In each case, his entry was officially a private one, but Cricklewood assisted with the preparation of the cars and provided moral support. July saw him racing one of the team cars at the German Grand Prix, held at the Nurburgring. There was

---

THE 1928 TT CARS

Details of the 1928 TT cars were as follows:

Chassis no	Registration	Race no	Crew
KM3077	YV 7263	53	Tim Birkin
TX3246	YW 5758	54	Humphrey Cook

THE 1928 BOILLOT CUP CARS

Details of the 1928 Boillot Cup car were as follows:

Chassis no	Registration	Race no	Crew
KM3077	YV 7263	69	Tim Birkin

Then in August, Birkin was flying the Bentley flag again when he and Humphrey Cook, another gentleman amateur, entered 4½-litres in the Tourist Trophy race. As far as the works was concerned, these were again private entries; the 1928 rules allowed small-capacity cars to compete alongside the bigger ones, which were appropriately handicapped, and WO suspected that the resulting large number of entries would create "traffic" problems. He was right, but in spite of these problems Birkin placed fifth, and Cook came seventh. Finally, Birkin took his 4½-litre to Boulogne for the annual Georges Boillot Cup in September. Though he finished in fifth place, he also beat all existing records for the race with an average speed of 73.16mph.

1929 – the greatest triumph

While Birkin believed that supercharging was the way forward, WO was convinced that a more powerful six-cylinder engine would keep the Bentley marque ahead, and to that end was working on the car that became the Speed Six. However, he was far from done with the 4½-litre yet, and planned the 1929 Bentley assault on Le Mans around a team of two 4½-litres plus an experimental Speed Six.

First, though, was the annual dress rehearsal,

A pit stop for the eventual 1928 Le Mans winner, car number 4.

works involvement of course, and his riding mechanic was Cricklewood's Wally Hassan. He finished a disappointing eighth in a race that was dominated by the supercharged Mercedes cars. As Chapter 6 explains, it was this experience which determined him to look into supercharging the Bentley engine to keep the car competitive.

Barnato and Rubin with their 4½-litre after winning the 1928 Le Mans. Their expressions seem to convey a mixture of triumph and exhaustion.

Different lighting arrangements again: the Clement-Chassagne car on its way to fourth place in the 1929 Le Mans event, where the new Speed Six Bentley was overall winner.

and this year the event that Cricklewood chose was the Double Twelve at Brooklands, a new fixture organized by the Junior Car Club. This was ideally placed in the calendar over the weekend of 10-11 May; the Six Hours race that the team had used before was this year not run until June. One Speed Six was entered, driven by Woolf Barnato and Dudley Benjafield, but it was put out of the race by a failed dynamo drive while in the lead. The other four Bentleys in the event were all 4½-litres, two being "works" entries and two being privateers. Of the privateers, Birkin and Holder did not finish, but Scott (partnered by his wife) came a creditable 11th. Clement and Cook in one of the "works" cars retired after running a big end, but Sammy Davis, partnered with Roland Gunter, came second.

But before Le Mans, Bentley would make one more attempt on the 24-hour record at Montlhéry – or rather, they would support an extremely courageous and talented lady driver of the time to do so. Mary Petre normally used her maiden name when racing but she was also the Hon Mrs Victor Bruce, and she was a very persuasive person. She persuaded Barnato and WO to allow her to tackle the record with the "works" 4½-litre that Tim Birkin had driven in the 1928 Le Mans (chassis number KM3077).

The timing, as had so often happened before, turned out to be tricky. Mary Petre's attempt on the record was booked in for early June. The original plan was for Tim Birkin to enter two

supercharged 4½-litres for Le Mans under his own name, which was why his unsupercharged car was available for the record runs. However, as Chapter 4 shows, the supercharged cars gave problems at the very last minute and had to be withdrawn. Unwilling to risk the negative publicity that would result from the withdrawal of two Bentley cars, even though they were not

THE 1929 DOUBLE TWELVE CARS

Details of the 1929 Double Twelve cars were as follows:

Chassis no	Registration	Race no	Crew
KM3077	YV 3263	5	Frank Clement and Humphrey Cook
KM3088	YW 2557	6	Sammy Davis and Roland Gunter
NX3451	UU 5580	10	WB "Bummer" Scott and Jill Scott
FB3301	UL 4471	12	Tim Birkin and Nigel Holder

Note: The fifth Bentley entry in this event was a Speed Six driven by Woolf Barnato and Dudley Benjafield, running as no 2.

THE 1929 MONTLHÉRY RECORD CAR

Details of the 1929 Montlhéry record car were as follows:

Chassis no	Registration	Race no	Crew
KM3077	YV 7263	(N/A)	Mary Petre

The changing shape of the sports-racer: the Clement-Chassagne car looks positively old-fashioned as it closes in on the 999cc Bourcier-Tribaudot Tracta, which is emitting a worrying quantity of smoke and later retired. Ettore Bugatti's supposed jibe that Bentley built the world's fastest lorries seems quite appropriate!

THE 1929 LE MANS CARS

Details of the 1929 Le Mans cars were as follows:

Chassis no	Registration	Race no	Crew
TX3246	YW 5758	8	Frank Clement and Jean Chassagne
ST3001	YH 3196	9	Glen Kidston and Jack Dunfee
KM3088	YW 2557	10	Dudley Benjafield and André d'Erlanger
KM3077	YV 3263	11	Bernard Rubin and Earl Howe

Note: The fifth Bentley entry in this event (and the winner) was a Speed Six driven by Woolf Barnato and Tim Birkin, running as no 1.

THE 1929 SIX HOURS CARS

Details of the 1929 Six Hours cars were as follows:

Chassis no	Registration	Race no	Crew
TX3246	YW 5758	4	Humphrey Cook and Leslie Callingham
HB3402 Supercharged	UU 5871	5	Tim Birkin
FB3301	UL 4471	6	Nigel Holder
NX3451	UU 5580	7	WB "Bummer" Scott and Patterson

Note: The fifth Bentley entry in this event was a Speed Six driven by Woolf Barnato and Jack Dunfee, running as no 3.

"works" entries, WO and Barnato agreed to replace them with two additional 4½-litre "works" entries. One of the cars they planned to use was the one already earmarked for Mary Petre's record attempt.

The plan was for the "record" car to be driven to Montlhéry by two Bentley mechanics along with a representative from the Shell petrol company, who also had an interest in the event. Once the record runs were over, the car would be driven straight down to Le Mans for the 24-hour race. However, in an excess of exuberance, the Shell representative drove the car into a tree on the way to Montlhéry, buckling the chassis frame and the front axle. After some urgent telephone calls, the necessary parts were shipped across the Channel and the car was repaired at a Boulogne garage, ready for Mary Petre to use. And use it she did, taking the record for a single-handed 24-hour drive by covering 2164 miles at an average speed of more than 89mph. The car, apparently no worse for its recent experiences, was then delivered to Le Mans.

As Chapter 6 explains, Tim Birkin had entered two of his supercharged cars under his own name for Le Mans, but last-minute problems led to both being withdrawn. Bentley Motors stepped in – perhaps with the idea of upholding their own name as much as anything else – and took the two vacant positions on the grid with a

Visible in this picture from the 1929 Le Mans are the Kidston-Dunfee car, number 9, and the Benjafield-d'Erlanger car, number 10. Car number 2 is a Du Pont, number 6 a Stutz. By the Sunday, all the Bentley entries had been slowed down, on WO's orders.

pair of "works" 4½-litres at the last minute. This led to a reshuffle of drivers. Birkin himself was allocated as Barnato's co-driver in the Speed Six. Frank Clement and Jean Chassagne shared car no 8, and there were two new drivers in car no 9, the original 4½-litre prototype. These were Glen Kidston, a wealthy distinguished former naval commander and pioneer aviator, and Jack Dunfee, an experienced Brooklands regular. Dudley Benjafield and André d'Erlanger shared the 4½-litre that Benjafield had driven with Clement in the 1928 Le Mans, running as number 10, and the Petre record car ran as number 11 with Bernard Rubin (another wealthy Bentley-owning friend of Barnato's) and Earl Howe (Francis Curzon, the fifth Earl and another gentleman amateur) as crew.

The first Bentley to drop out of the running on 15 June was the Howe-Rubin car, although not for reasons directly related to its eventful recent history. A fibre distributor gear on one of the magnetos stripped, and when it was replaced somebody forgot to fit a vital gasket. As a result, oil leaked, and the magneto cross-shaft seized and broke. Car number 11 was out on the seventh lap.

Car number 10, driven by Benjafield and d'Er-langer, developed electrical difficulties when the inter-cell connecting lug on the off-side battery fractured. Then, towards the end of the race, it developed a severe water leak from the pump

Dudley Benjafield and André d'Erlanger were partnered twice in Bentleys for major events. The first time was in a 4½-litre for the 1929 Le Mans, when they claimed third place; the second was in a supercharged car for the 1930 Double Twelve, when their car retired with back axle failure.

THE 1929 IRISH GRAND PRIX CARS

Details of the 1929 Irish Grand Prix cars were as follows:

Chassis no	Registration	Race no	Crew
HB3402	UU 5871	2	Tim Birkin
Supercharged			
HB3403	UU5872	3	Bernard Rubin
Supercharged			
KM3077	YV 3263	7	Beris Harcourt-Wood
FB3301	UL 4471	8	Nigel Holder
TX3246	YW 5758	9	Humphrey Cook
NX3451	UU 5580	10	WB "Bummer" Scott

Note: The seventh Bentley entry in this event was a Speed Six driven by Glen Kidston, running as no 4.

THE 1929 TT CARS

Details of the 1929 TT cars were as follows:

Chassis no	Registration	Race no	Crew
HB3402	UU 5871	63	Tim Birkin and WO Bentley
Supercharged			
HB3403	UU5872	64	Bernard Rubin
Supercharged			
HB3404/R	YU3250	65	Beris Harcourt-Wood
Supercharged			
ST3001	YH 3196	66	Hayes and Field

Note: The fifth Bentley entry in this event was a Speed Six driven by Glen Kidston, running as no 73.

THE 1929 BROOKLANDS 500 CARS

Details of the 1929 Brooklands 500 cars were as follows:

Chassis no	Registration	Race no	Crew
TX3246	YW 5758	31	Jack Barclay and Frank Clement
HB3402	UU 5871	32	Tim Birkin and Beris Harcourt-Wood
Supercharged			
NX3541	UU 5580	33	Tim Rose-Richards and CW "Turkey" Fiennes
ST3001	YH 3196	34	Jack Dunfee

Note: The fifth Bentley entry in this event was a Speed Six driven by Sammy Davis and Clive Dunfee, running as no 35.

gland. Unfortunately, nobody realised that the pump only leaked when the engine was stopped for refuelling in the pits and did not do so when the engine was running. As a result, a lot of valuable time was wasted trying to stop the leak.

Le Mans regulations this year demanded that the weight of two passengers was carried in each car as ballast, and the Bentleys carried lead in a steel tube fixed ahead of the radiator. Frank Clement in car number 8 lost valuable time when the ballast he was carrying shifted: the security bolts anchoring the tube that contained the ballast stretched, and the movement distorted the body-frame which then fouled the front brake mechanism. Kidston in car number 9 had his oil filler overflow gear come adrift.

And yet, despite these difficulties, Le Mans 1929 ended as Bentley's greatest triumph. The cars achieved a commanding lead and in the interests of reliability WO ordered the 4½-litres to slow down for the last two hours of the race; the Speed Six was instructed to slow down for the last 12 hours. According to Sammy Davis's memoir, *Motor Racing*, Jack Dunfee actually got out of his car at one point and went for a drink at a local café in order to keep to his time schedule! Of the five cars that Cricklewood entered, four finished – and they took the top four places in the event. The winner was the Barnato-Birkin Speed Six; second were Kidston and Dunfee, third Benjafield and d'Erlanger, and fourth were Clement and Chassagne. In fifth place, and a good three laps behind Clement and Chassagne's Bentley, was the supercharged Stutz of Guy Bouriat and Philippe de Rothschild.

Of course, there were more Bentley entries in major events later that year. The Six Hours race at Brooklands, now organized by the BARC rather than the Essex Car Club as in previous years and not held until 29 June, attracted five Bentley entries. With perseverance, Birkin's team had been able to get a supercharged car ready to run in this event. Birkin himself drove, and as expected, the car proved much faster than the "works" 4½-litres. However, Birkin did not finish, retiring for undisclosed reasons. Holder's unblown 4½-litre also gave in to engine failure and did not finish. However, of the other 4½-litres, Scott and Patterson claimed 8th place and Cook and Callingham finished third. The winning car was the Speed Six, driven by Barnato and Jack Dunfee.

A couple of weeks later, on 13 July, no fewer than seven Bentleys were down as starters for the Irish Grand Prix at Phoenix Park. Two were supercharged 4½-litres from the Birkin-Paget team, and one was a Speed Six, with Glen Kidston at the wheel. Predictably, perhaps, the Speed Six did best of all, finishing in second place. It seemed as though WO might have been right to put his faith in the bigger-engined car after all.

Nevertheless, the other Bentleys were far from disgraced. Leaving aside the Holder 4½-litre, which failed to start, the other five finished right behind the Speed Six in third, fourth, fifth, seventh and eighth places, separated by an Alfa Romeo in sixth position. Birkin claimed third place, and Bernard Rubin in the second supercharged car was eighth, both cars having amply demonstrated the cooling deficiencies of the original supercharged design.

The TT, run on 17 August, attracted five Bentley entries. Three were the supercharged cars of the Birkin team, one an unblown 4½-litre, and one a Speed Six driven by Kidston, which was a "works" entry despite Cricklewood's official withdrawal from racing. Of particular interest was that WO himself rode with Birkin as his mechanic in a supercharged car. One story had it that he had done so with the aim of setting an example to the Bentley mechanics, who had been muttering that the TT was a dangerous event. However, he later admitted that the experience was one of the most frightening of his life.

That year's TT race was run in appalling weather; three cars were put out of the running by accidents, the unblown 4½-litre was flagged off after a wheel collapsed, and only Birkin finished – in a disappointing 11th place on handicap, although he was second on pure speed. The winner was the German ace Rudolf Caracciola, in a supercharged Mercedes.

The last major event of 1929 was a little more encouraging, however. At the Brooklands 500 Miles Race, held on 12 October and the first of its kind, all the cars were stripped for the track, shedding wings, lights and other items. Of the five entries – one, predictably, a Birkin team

"blower" – three finished. Jack Barclay and Frank Clement took first place on handicap in a 4½-litre which had been modified with a pointed tail; Sammy Davis and Clive Dunfee placed second in a Speed Six; and Rose-Richards and Fiennes claimed fifth place in a 4½-litre borrowed from Scott. The Birkin "blower" retired when a flexible joint in its outside exhaust disintegrated.

1930 – passing the baton

However, the days of the four-cylinder Bentley's successes in international events were over. While Birkin ploughed his own furrow with the supercharged 4½-litre without success, the "works" team went over completely to six-cylinder cars. The change was short-lived: shortly after the 1930 Le Mans – where Speed Six Bentleys claimed first and second places –

THE 1930 TT CARS

Details of the 1930 TT cars were as follows:

Chassis no	Registration	Race no	Crew
HB3403	UU5872	1	Tim Birkin
Supercharged			
HB3404/R	YU3250	2	Bertie Kensington-Moir
Supercharged			
HR3976	UR 6571	3	Dudley Benjafield
Supercharged			
DS3556	UV 3108	4	Eddie Hall

THE 1930 DOUBLE TWELVE CARS

Details of the four-cylinder Bentleys that raced in the 1930 Double Twelve were as follows:

Chassis no	Registration	Race no	Crew
HB3403	UU5872	4	Tim Birkin and
Supercharged			Jean Chassagne
HB3404/R	YU3250	5	Glen Kidston and
Supercharged			Jack Dunfee
HR3976	UR 6571	6	Dudley Benjafield and
Supercharged			André d'Erlanger
FT3209	YW 8936	10	MO de B Durand and
			TK Williams

Note: The fifth and sixth Bentley entries in this event were both Speed Six models. Frank Clement and Wolf Barnato drove car no 2 (and won); Sammy Davis and Clive Dunfee drove car no 3 (and came second).

Le Mans 1930 was the year of the Speed Six as far as Bentley Motors were concerned, but it was also the year of the Birkin supercharged cars. Speed Six number 3 and Birkin "blower" number 7 are seen here at the traditional start as drivers sprint across the track to their waiting cars.

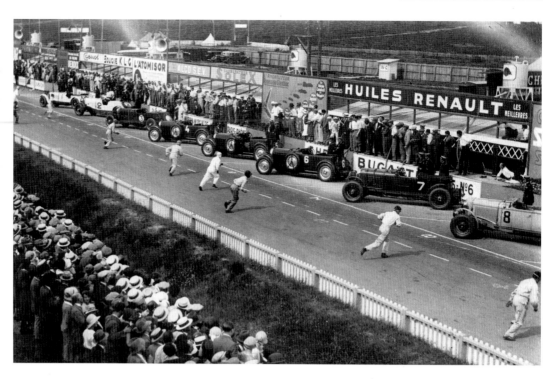

THE 1930 LE MANS CARS

Details of the 1930 Le Mans four-cylinder Bentleys were as follows:

Chassis no	Registration	Race no	Crew
HB3404/R	YU3250	7	Jack Dunfee and
Supercharged			Beris Harcourt-Wood
HR3976	UR 6571	8	Giulio Ramponi and
Supercharged			Dudley Benjafield
HB3403	UU5872	9	Tim Birkin and
Supercharged			Jean Chassagne

Note: Three Speed Six Bentleys also entered for this event. The Sammy Davis/Clive Dunfee car (no 3) did not finish, but the Clement/Watney car (no 2) came second and the race was won by Woolf Barnato and Glen Kidston driving car no 4.

THE 1930 IRISH GP CARS

Details of the 1930 Irish GP cars were as follows:

Chassis no	Registration	Race no	Crew
HB3404/R	YU3250	6	Beris Harcourt-Wood
Supercharged			
HR3976	UR 6571	7	Jean Chassagne
Supercharged			
HB3403	UU5872	8	Tim Birkin
Supercharged			

The Clement-Watney Speed Six, car number 2, leads the Ramponi-Benjafield "blower" at Le Mans in 1930.

These two shots of the Ramponi-Benjafield supercharged car show it in action at Le Mans in 1930. A collapsed piston eventually put the car out of the race.

the Bentley "works" team withdrew from racing. It was, quite simply, too expensive for the company to continue fielding an internationally competitive team in the face of increasing financial difficulties. Nevertheless, some of the former "works" team cars continued to appear in major motorsport events over the next few years.

However, the official withdrawal from racing did not affect Tim Birkin and his operation in Welwyn Garden City. As Chapter 6 explains, he had secured funding from the Hon Dorothy Paget, and this helped him keep his "blowers" on the racetracks during 1930. As soon as the money became available at the end of 1929, Birkin had set to work to put his racing stable on a more professional footing. Supercharged car No 1 was rebodied as a single-seater by Thomson & Taylor at Brooklands, and was on test there by March 1930. Car No 2 was rebuilt on a short chassis, losing 13 inches in the process. A second short-chassis car was built up and became the No 4 car. It also took the first number (HR 3976) of the 25 chassis numbers that had been allocated to Birkin to build his supercharged racers.

During 1930, Birkin did his damnedest, racing under the banner of the Hon Dorothy Paget team. On 9-10 May, he entered three cars for the Double Twelve event at Brooklands, a 24-hour

THE 1930 BROOKLANDS 500 CARS

Details of the 1930 French GP car were as follows:

Chassis no	Registration	Race no	Crew
HB3402	UU 5871	36	Tim Birkin and
Supercharged			George Duller
HR3976	UR 6571	37	George Eyston and
Supercharged			Beris Harcourt-Wood
HB3403	UU5872	38	Eddie Hall and
Supercharged			Dudley Benjafield

Birkin was not going to let tyre problems trouble him at Le Mans in 1930, and kept driving hard when they arose. As a result, a tyre disintegrated and wrecked the rear wing, and Birkin lost valuable time getting the car raceworthy again. Only drivers were allowed to work on the cars during the race – which is why the pit crew seem to be taking it easy.

Roland Gunter partnered Sammy Davis in a 4½-litre in the 1930 Double Twelve event at Brooklands.

race divided into two daylight stretches of 12 hours. Jack Dunfee in car No 3 retired with a broken valve; Birkin retired in car No 2 with a cracked chassis frame; and Benjafield in car No 1 retired with back axle failure. In a further vindication of WO's insistence on larger capacity

as a way to reliable extra power, first and second places were taken by "works" Speed Sixes.

Birkin was there alongside the "works" team at the 1930 Le Mans on 21 and 22 June, too, when he entered three cars. It was of course his determination to enter a supercharged Bentley at Le Mans which had led to the need for a production run of 50, and which had caused so much friction with WO. Birkin's own car, shared with Jean Chassagne, broke a con-rod, but not before it had set a new lap record. A collapsed piston put the second car, driven by Benjafield and the former Alfa Romeo driver Giulio Ramponi, out of contention. It was true that one of the "works" Speed Sixes crashed and had to retire, but the other two took first and second places.

Then, with Bentley Motors no longer officially competing, it is arguable that the Birkin-Paget team took over the Bentley mantle on the international race tracks. Several former "works" drivers drove for them, as indeed they had in the days when they were also engaged as "works" team drivers. On 19 July, the Birkin-Paget team entered the Irish Grand Prix in Dublin. They lost Chassagne's and Harcourt-Wood's cars to lubrication problems. Birkin's car

Tim Birkin was nothing if not determined. After securing sponsorship from the Hon Dorothy Paget, he had the first "blower" rebodied as a single-seater, and is seen here at the wheel.

THE 1930 FRENCH GP CAR

Details of the 1930 French GP car were as follows:

Chassis no	Registration	Race no	Crew
HR3976	UR 6571	18	Tim Birkin
Supercharged			

developed similar difficulties, but he nursed it to a very creditable fourth place. Then, at the Tourist Trophy event on 23 August, Birkin crashed, the Benjafield/Chassagne car failed to complete the required number of laps, and Bertie Kensington-Moir returned the best result in 11th place. Birkin himself took the single-seater to a splendid second place in the French Grand Prix at Pau in September, and then in the 500 Miles race at Brooklands in October, the Hall/Benjafield car claimed second place, although Birkin's single-seater was misfiring badly and was unplaced, while the Eyston/Harcourt-Wood car retired with a broken magneto drive.

It was a patchy set of results, and not enough to convince Dorothy Paget that she should plough more of her money into the Birkin team. She withdrew her sponsorship at the end of 1930, although Birkin persuaded her to retain the single-seater and to let him race it at Brooklands – which he did until his death three years later.

... and the private entries

Even though Bentley Motors officially withdrew from racing shortly after the 1930 Le Mans event, Tim Birkin's racing outfit was still at liberty to race Bentleys. As Chapter 6 explains, however, his results during the rest of 1930 were disappointing, and for 1931 he found himself without the financial support from Dorothy Paget which had kept him going in 1930. A Le Mans entry in 1931 would have been beyond his means, and he made none.

None of that prevented enthusiastic amateurs from doing their best to keep the Bentley flag flying at Le Mans and elsewhere, and one of the former "works" 4½-litres was pressed into service for a private entry in the 1931 Le Mans event, while a Birkin "blower" contested the

Though there were no "works" entries in the 1931 Le Mans, one of the ex-team 4½-litres was campaigned with some spirit by Bevan and Couper.

THE 1931 LE MANS CAR

Details of the 1931 Le Mans car were as follows:

Chassis no	Registration	Race no	Crew
KM3077	YV 3263	7	Anthony Bevan and Mike Couper

THE 1931 BROOKLANDS 500 CARS

Details of the 1931 Brooklands 500 cars were as follows:

Chassis no	Registration	Race no	Crew
HB3402	UU 5871	42	Dudley Benjafield
KM3077	YV 3263	43	Anthony Bevan and Mike Couper

Note: A third Bentley entry was a Speed Six driven by Jack Dunfee and Cyril Paul, racing as no 46.

For 1932, an ex-Birkin "blower" tackled Le Mans in the hands of Jean Trevoux and "Mary" – but without success.

Trevoux, this time paired with Louis Gas, again had race number 5 in the 1933 Le Mans and again campaigned the ex-Birkin "blower".

THE 1932 LE MANS CAR

Details of the 1932 Le Mans car were as follows:

Chassis no	Registration	Race no	Crew
HR3976	UR 6571	5	Jean Trevoux and "Mary"
Supercharged			

THE 1933 LE MANS CAR

Details of the 1933 Le Mans car were as follows:

Chassis no	Registration	Race no	Crew
HR3976	UR 6571	5	Jean Trevoux and Louis Gas
Supercharged			

1932 and 1933 Le Mans. Two former "works" 4½-litres featured in the 1931 Brooklands 500 race. None of these entries, unfortunately, made a mark. The days of the Bentleys as an international force in racing were over, as faster cars took the lead and, without the organization and determination which had been behind the "works" entries of the late 1920s, their chances of success were always going to be very slim.

The Le Mans specification 4½-litre Bentley
By the time the 4½-litre models entered the Bentley "works" team, Cricklewood had given up the pretence of racing with production-standard or nearly production-standard cars. In order to remain competitive with the dedicated racing machinery fielded by other manufacturers, they had to use specially prepared cars. So although the "works" racing Bentleys (record-breakers apart) looked pretty much like the open four-seaters that were on sale to the general public, they were in fact rather different.

Their chassis and engines were carefully prepared in the Racing Shop at Cricklewood under the supervision of Frank Clement, and their bodywork was specially made by Vanden Plas. Between 1927 and 1929, there were just eight Le Mans specification cars, of which four were genuine "works" team cars and the other four were produced to special order for private owners with the full Le Mans specification.

Chapter Ten

Afterlife

This book has deliberately presented a picture of the vintage Bentleys when they were new: why they were the way they were, what they looked like, and how people saw them at the time. But more than 90 years have passed since WO and his colleagues put their first 3-litre prototype on the road, and more than 80 years since the last car left the Cricklewood factory. In all that time, a major transformation has taken place.

Probably the most striking aspects of that transformation, as far as the modern enthusiast is concerned, are the huge increase in the value of the cars and the equally huge reduction in the variety of vintage Bentleys that have survived. The purchase price of a top-quality vintage Bentley in original condition – or as original as it can reasonably be after eight decades – now far exceeds its purchase price when new, even allowing for the changing value of money in that period.

As for the loss of variety, it is best understood by asking the stereotypical man on the Clapham omnibus what he imagines when he thinks of a vintage Bentley. The chances are that his vision involves an open tourer, quite possibly supercharged, and most definitely painted in British Racing Green. The notion that there were ever any other body options usually comes as a surprise.

The issue of the cars' escalating prices really needs very little comment. The vintage Bentley continues to attract enthusiasm and interest, and prices have been driven upwards by the laws of supply and demand: a lot of people would like to own a fairly small number of cars, and so sellers inevitably sell to the one who bids highest. The question of that reduction in variety, however, needs more careful explanation.

First of all, there is absolutely no doubt that the sporting successes of the marque, particularly at Le Mans, left an indelible impression on the public. Vintage Bentleys remained popular in club racing during the 1930s, even though they were no longer competitive in international events, and demand for the sporting variants remained strong. There was, perhaps understandably, much less demand for those cars with more formal bodywork. Their bodies were

The RC-series cars were particularly interesting, as they combined what were effectively 1920s chassis with 1930s bodywork. This one is RC32, built in 1936 on a reconditioned chassis by Bentley Motors (1931) Ltd and fitted with a contemporary Vanden Plas drophead body derived from that company's design for the "Derby" Bentleys of the time.

This short-chassis 3-litre seems to have been rebodied in the early 1930s by Abbott of Farnham, who opened for business in 1929. Rebodying a car that was still relatively young was not uncommon as chassis outlasted all but the very best coachwork in those days.

to them. So, for example, they rebuilt a number of otherwise "ordinary" supercharged models (if any of those can really be called ordinary) with Le Mans extras.

Demand continued into the middle of the decade, and this time it was HM Bentley & Partners, the company run by WO's older brother, who added modification to the activities of their car sales business. Broadly speaking, the HM Bentley rebuilds kept within the spirit of the original (sporting) cars, but added a few more modern features that appealed to the customers of the time. In some cases, cars were re-engined, a 3-litre for example being given more performance with the substitution of a 4½-litre engine.

heavy enough to rob the cars of performance; the cars were no longer new and fashionable enough to attract buyers in the carriage trade for which they had originally been built (and besides, that trade itself was changing); and it was prohibitively expensive for private owners to maintain or repair the hand-finished bespoke coachwork as their timber frames rotted and fixings loosened.

Some companies capitalised on the interest in sporting Bentleys from a very early stage. Most notable in the early 1930s were Birkin & Couper, Tim Birkin's race preparation outfit in Welwyn Garden City. Before Birkin's untimely death in 1933, they probably saw themselves as continuing the great tradition of the Racing Shop at Cricklewood. They prepared customers' cars, and in particular they modified them to meet whatever sporting requirement a customer put

All this helped to keep interest in the original cars alive, even though the cars now being produced under the Bentley name had some very different characteristics. Rolls-Royce, who had bought Bentley Motors in 1931, decided to capitalise on this in 1935-36 and to clear some stocks of 1920s Bentley parts at the same time. So it was that ten "new" chassis were constructed – four 3-litres and six 4½-litres – from reconditioned and new parts. The ten chassis were bodied in the contemporary idiom, mostly as drophead coupés of one sort or another, and found a ready market.

Meanwhile, those who campaigned the Bentleys of the 1920s in club events needed a cheap source of spares. As prices began to fall, and the less serviceable cars were taken off the road, so it became viable to buy a second complete car as a source of parts. More engine swaps were carried out. Sometimes chassis frames might be swapped, and in many cases there was never any official notification of the change.

This is the kind of thing that old-car enthusiasts have always done and will probably always continue to do, but it did lead to the creation of

One of those mysteries. This seems to be chassis 574, which was supposedly destroyed in the fire in 1924 at the Gurney Nutting coachworks. The registration number it carries here could not have been issued before September 1933. The chassis looks suspiciously short, so perhaps the car was shortened as well as given a contemporary drophead coupé body in the 1930s.
The picture dates from the Second World War, when cars were obliged to wear headlamp masks during the night-time blackout.

many cars that were not "authentic" in the sense that they were as Bentley Motors had made them.

Most importantly, at least as far as modern perceptions of the vintage Bentley are concerned, the surviving cars were not revered in the way that they are today. They were a source of fun – and the cheaper that fun, the better. Expensive coachbuilt bodies in need of repair were simply discarded, and in their place was fitted minimalist racing bodywork.

Then came the war. Petrol was strictly rationed, and many cars were laid up for the duration either for that reason or because their owners were serving in the armed forces and were no longer able to use them. There was a demand for metal, and a vintage Bentley that did not run and had rotten bodywork became more attractive as two tons of scrap metal than as a motor car. So a good number of cars must have disappeared in this period.

It was some time before things returned to normal after the end of the war. In a time of rationing and austerity, motor racing was seen as a luxury that the country could not afford. Prices of 1920s Bentleys dropped still lower, cars that had survived were often neglected, and more examples passed the point of no return where they were simply not worth restoring.

Very many cars have been rebuilt and modified over the years, and saloon bodies have been replaced by sporting four-seaters as they have become due for replacement. This is an April 1927 3-litre, on chassis number BL1624, and was fitted with a Harrison saloon body when new.

The 1950s saw a return of enthusiasm, but prices were still generally low. Nobody thought twice about making one good car out of two or three others. Yet interest was rising: in 1958, WO Bentley published his autobiography, and over the next few years he also put his name to a small number of other books that looked at the days of the vintage Bentley.

By the 1970s, prices and interest had begun to pick up again. Interest in older cars generally was on the increase, and among those older cars the vintage Bentleys were seen as elder statesmen worthy of an appropriate amount of respect. In 1976, Stanley Sedgwick, the President of the Bentley Drivers' Club, published the first edition of his classic compilation, *All the pre-war Bentleys – as new*. It covered the

Sporting events have always been a particular focus for vintage Bentley enthusiasts, and this picture from the Bentley Drivers' Club archives shows one of the club's track events. The car in the centre is a 1923 3-litre, now running a 4½-litre engine, while in front of it and being driven with some élan is a Bentley 8-litre.

3-litre chassis number 290, since scrapped. Its components are now to be found in various cars.

manufactured 80 or 90 years ago. It is said, in fact, that you could now build a complete vintage Bentley from replica parts – including the chassis frame! While this is excellent news for the genuine enthusiast, and means that no vintage Bentley need be put out of commission for want of a vital part, it is also excellent news for those who might wish to pass off a car as something it is not. There are, as there always have been, unscrupulous sellers as well as reputable and honest sellers. The really unfortunate side to this is that the genuine honest seller may be tarred with the same brush as the dishonest one.

What is fortunate is that enormously detailed records of most vintage Bentleys still survive. Before thinking seriously about the purchase of a car, any enthusiast should check the records held at the Bentley Drivers' Club (www.bdcl.org); they are likely to include not only the original build record but also the records of when early owners had the car serviced by Bentley. There may also be old photographs and documents which previous owners have donated to the club for its archives. More than one owner of a supposedly all-original car has been somewhat dismayed to discover from these records that, actually, his car was given a new chassis frame after an accident when it was five or so years old.

Unlike newer classic cars, vintage Bentleys generally do not get everyday use. They are too valuable to leave unattended (vandals have no respect for a car's age), and although capable of keeping up with modern traffic they are not the easiest machines to manoeuvre. It used to be said that a vintage Bentley was a man's car and, although the company used to print many testimonials from satisfied lady drivers in its sales catalogues during the 1920s, it is not hard to see why this description should have come about in an age when a car's controls generally became much lighter and easier to manage.

The first obstacle is that the pedals are arranged differently from the current norm (and some owners have changed them to the modern

"Derby" Bentleys up to 1940 as well as the "WO" cars that had established the marque in the 1920s, but it did indicate that there was now a real interest in the authentic history of the Bentley. Its approach – an attempt to go back to the origins of the cars and make clear how much had changed – has influenced writers about the 1920s cars ever since.

Buying a vintage Bentley today, assuming the funds are available, can be a real minefield. The cars' prices – and the sums of money that some owners are willing to spend in restoration costs – mean that specialists are willing to replicate almost any part for one of these cars. Many of these replicas are so good that they are virtually indistinguishable from original Bentley parts

This 1924 3-litre, on chassis number 549, is again representative of the afterlife of many vintage Bentleys. Built in 1924 on a 10ft 10in wheelbase, it was cut down to 9ft 9½in in the 1950s and fitted with open sporting bodywork and the cycle wings typical of cars from the later 1920s.

pattern to make the cars easier to drive). The second is that the gearchange can be difficult, and the third that the steering can be very heavy at low speeds. The biggest obstacle, though, is other drivers. Sadly, few have the imagination or the manners to recognise that the dynamics of an 80-year-old car are not the same as those of a modern one, and fail to make allowances.

Die-hard enthusiasts enjoy the challenge that all this represents, and there is no doubt that mastering the art of driving a vintage Bentley can be enormously satisfying. Watching other drivers hurling these large and apparently unwieldy machines around a race track – as happens at the BDC's annual Silverstone meeting – can also be immensely enjoyable, and can give a flavour of the days of Brooklands and Le Mans. Either ectivity is heartily recommended as an adjunct to reading this book and its companion volume.

The 1936 RC series chassis
The story behind the ten RC-series chassis that were created in 1936 is more one of business acumen than of sentiment for the products of the old Bentley Motors. The new Rolls-Royce-owned company wanted to make use of the

Several of the RC-series chassis received these rather attractive Vanden Plas bodies in 1936, which were quite different from those typically fitted in the heyday of the "WO" Bentleys. This is chassis number RC44.

huge quantity of spares it had bought along with the rights to the Bentley name, and one very good way of doing so was to turn them into as many complete cars as they could manufacture. Nobby Clarke, who had been the foreman at Cricklewood and later the Works Superintendent, was still on the strength, and he was given the task of creating the chassis; four of them were 3-litres, and the other six were 4½-litres.

The 3-litres were built over the summer of 1936 at the rate of about one a month to a specification which incorporated elements from the final Bentley models of more than one type: so they had SU electric fuel pumps rather than an Autovac, late C-type gearboxes, 4½-litre rear

Another vintage four-cylinder being used in the way WO intended, again at a BDC track event. Only the crash helmet tells us that this picture is a modern one.

Chassis 905 from November 1924 was a Speed Model – note the red background to the winged-B badge on the grille surround.

Not every vintage Bentley gets regular use, of course. This July 1924 Speed Model on chassis 733 was fitted when new with a four-seater body by Albany and has spent very many years on display in museums. It was pictured at the Atwell-Wilson Motor Museum in Calne in 2010.

were not recorded.

They were described as second-hand when supplied through JC Neville of the Service Sales Department. All four cars were given two-door four-seater drophead coupé bodies by Vanden Plas in a mid-1930s idiom, using a style derived from the one they had prepared for the contemporary Derby Bentleys. They were given new chassis numbers RC31 to RC34, the RC being generally understood as standing for "ReConditioned".

The six "new" 4½-litre cars had broadly similar different origins. Once again, it was Nobby Clarke, Service Works Manager under the Rolls-Royce-owned company, who had the responsibility of assembling them. These six chassis were something of a hotch-potch of parts that had been stored at the Bentley Service Station in Kingsbury. They, too, were given RC-prefix chassis numbers, in this case RC41 to RC46.

In theory, all were based on new-old-stock frames, but Michael Hay has identified the chassis of RC42 as having originally been DS3570, an accident-damaged 1929 4½-litre chassis which was removed and replaced in 1934. All six cars had late-type heavy-crank engines with Specialloid pistons, and D-type gearboxes which Hay says were taken from stock for the 4½-litre supercharged cars. They

axles, and the Dewandre vacuum servo brakes as seen on the 6½-litre and 8-litre chassis. The four chassis were actually old frames that had been bought in and reconditioned with new parts as required. All were on the 9ft 9½in wheelbase chassis, but their original identities

---

IDENTIFYING A VINTAGE BENTLEY

You will find the chassis number of a four-cylinder model stamped into the left-hand side of the chassis front cross-member and (usually) on the gearbox front cross member.

The engine number is stamped into the starter motor housing and (usually) into the magneto cross-shaft housing.

However, please remember that these numbers are only the beginning of the identification process!

More modifications: GF 3372 had chassis number XF3508 and was delivered in November 1929 as a 4½-litre with Vanden Plas four-seater sports body. Over the years it has acquired a supercharger.

had Speed Six rear axles with the 3.53:1 ratio, the later "heavy" front axle with the so-called servo brakes, and a 4-litre steering column modified to fit.

Five of the cars were bodied by Vanden Plas as four-seat tourers in the same mid-1930s idiom used for the RC-series 3-litre chassis. The sixth was bodied as a saloon by Corsica. All six of them were sold by JC Neville. They seem to have had only a one-year guarantee instead of the old Bentley five-year guarantee, and (like the RC-series 3-litres) have traditionally been viewed with some suspicion by vintage Bentley enthusiasts. Darrell Berthon and Anthony Stamer had this to say about them in their Profile of the 4½-litre Bentley in the late 1960s:

"Although made from genuine parts manufactured by the old Company, they were really hybrids and not part of the original production. Though admirable cars with a fair performance, they looked a bit odd to the experienced eye, with their rather ponderous 1936-type bodies built by Vanden Plas… and these cars have never been regarded as true 'Vintage' Bentleys in the old tradition."

However, it is at least arguable that these cars have closer links to the old Bentley Motors than some more modern confections that have been built from the parts of several different cars and then fitted with a modern replica body!

Also dating from 1936 is this rebuild by HM Bentley and Partners, fairly typical of the company's style. The car is on Speed chassis number DE1206, dating from July 1926, and the body was originally by Vanden Plas.

Needs must when the devil drives….The switchbox on the 1927 HJ Mulliner 3-litre saloon illustrated in Chapter 4 was cannibalised from another car in the 1960s to keep this one going; the chassis number engraved on it reads TX 3227, which was a 1928 4½-litre!

Keeping a lovely old Bentley going….A pair of modern SUs has been fitted to the engine of the 1927 HJ Mulliner saloon.

Appendix: A QUICK GUIDE TO THE FOUR-CYLINDER BENTLEYS

3-LITRE MODELS

1922 season (from August 1921)
- One wheelbase only (9ft 9½in)
- Radiator lower than scuttle, with blue enamel badge
- Rear-wheel brakes only
- Smith 45VS carburettor

1923 season (from August 1922)
- Two wheelbase options: 9ft 9½in (Short Standard) and 10ft 10in (Long Standard)
- TT Replica model introduced
- B-type gearbox
- Smith-Bentley 45BVS carburettor

1924 season (from August 1923)
- 10ft 10in wheelbase now standard
- Speed Model introduced, with red enamel radiator badge
- Four-wheel brakes introduced

1925 season (from August 1924)
- Taller radiator, now level with scuttle (mid-season)
- Speed Model now with twin SU G5 carburettors (mid-season)
- 100mph or Supersports (March 1925); 9ft wheelbase, radiator tapered towards base, green enamel badge
- Light Touring model (July 1925) on 9ft 9½in chassis

1926 season (from August 1925)
- Short Standard chassis discontinued
- Long Standard chassis, Speed Model, Supersports and Light Touring models remain available

1927 season (from August 1926)
- C-type gearbox with special ratios for all 9ft *9 1/2 in chassis and some Long Standard models

1928 season (from August 1927)
- No changes

1929 season (from August 1928)
- No changes
- Production ends (summer 1929)

4½-LITRE MODELS

1928 season (from August 1927)
- 10ft 10in wheelbase standard; 9ft 9½ in wheelbase available but rare
- Twin G 5 carburettors
- C-type gearbox; the D-type from March 1928
- White enamel radiator badge

1929 season (from August 1928)
- Vertical HVG5 carburettors
- Plate-type clutch
- Gradual switch to Electron castings
- "Servo" (leading-and-trailing shoe) brakes
- Steel shell-type main engine bearings (summer 1929)

1930 season (from August 1929)
- Pulswell silencer
- Supercharged models from first quarter of 1930
- Heavy-crank engine (February 1930)

1931 season (from August 1930)
- No changes
- Production ends (summer 1931)

RADIATOR BADGES

Several myths have grown up around Bentley's use of differently coloured radiator badges for different models. These have been reinforced to some extent by the present company's use from the late 1990s of black, blue, green and red badges (or "labels") to distinguish different varieties of the same car.

It is questionable whether WO and his colleagues stuck as religiously to the "meanings" associated with the different coloured badges used on four-cylinder Bentleys as enthusiasts tend to believe. A further complication has been that radiators and associated badges were swapped from car to car, particularly during the period when the four-cylinders were so cheap that an enthusiast might buy two or three to build one good car from them all. In such circumstances, a good radiator was simply a good radiator, regardless of the colour of badge attached to it.

According to tradition, these were the "correct" colours for the four-cylinder cars – but the list below should not be taken as a definitive guide in the absence of hard evidence.

Blue	All "standard" 3-litre models, on short or long wheelbase, 1922-29
Red	Speed Model 3-litre
Green	100mph (Supersports) 3-litre Works team cars from 1928 A green badge was also used on some (possibly all) the 4½-litres raced privately in major races between 1928 and 1930, perhaps in emulation of the green badge used on the works team cars
White	All other 4½-litres and all supercharged 4½-litres